# Learning to Like Life
## A Tribute to Lowell Bennion

# Learning to Like Life

## A Tribute to Lowell Bennion

George B. Handley

2017

Proceeds from the sale of this book will be donated to the Birch Creek Service Ranch, which continues the spirit of what Lowell Bennion began and which needs your support. Read about BCSR at http://www.serviceranch.org/.

George B. Handley is a Professor of Interdisciplinary Humanities at Brigham Young University. His creative writing, literary criticism, and civic engagement focus on the intersection between religion, literature, and the environment. Other works include *American Fork* (2017; novel), *Home Waters: A Year of Recompenses on the Provo River* (2010; memoir), *Postcolonial Ecologies: Literatures of the Environment* (co-edited with Elizabeth DeLoughrey, 2011; academic), *New World Poetics: Nature and the Adamic Imagination in Whitman, Neruda, and Walcott* (2007; academic), *Caribbean Literature and the Environment: Between Nature and Culture* (co-edited with Elizabeth DeLoughrey and Renée Gosson, 2006; academic), *Stewardship and the Creation: LDS Perspectives on Nature* (co-edited with Terry Ball and Steven Peck, 2005; academic), and *Postslavery Literatures in the Americas: Family Portraits in Black and White* (2000; academic). More information available at www.georgebhandley.com.

ISBN-10: 1975992695
ISBN-13: 978-1975992699

Cover photo by George B. Handley, Aspen trees in Teton Valley, Idaho.

Author photo by Olivia Snow
oliviabrowningsnow.com

This text for this book uses Adobe Garamond, designed by Robert Slimbach for Adobe Systems and released in 1989. The titles are set in Myriad Pro, designed by Robert Slimbach and Carol Twombly for Adobe Systems and released in 2000.

Design by Jenny Webb
www.jennywebbedits.com

# Contents

# Preface

LOWELL BENNION (1908–1996) WAS A TREASURE. He was a brilliant intellectual and educator. His many books expressed a practical guide for keeping the gospel of Jesus Christ simple, applicable, and principled. He was loved by generations of students who came under his influence at the University of Utah because he offered a comprehensive and integrated approach to belief that assisted many with their doubts during a time of transition in the church. He was not afraid to speak his mind, least of all on behalf of the most disadvantaged, but he was more than a voice. He was one of the greatest humanitarians in the LDS tradition. He devoted decades of his life to volunteer service on behalf of those people within the range of his considerable reach whose lives he could improve, and he inspired countless others to take up the same opportunities. To Lowell Bennion, belief was a responsibility, not a privilege, a means and not an end, and it meant that we had to do the hard work of translating ideals into real practices that had measurable impact for good in the lives of those who suffered disproportionately the insults of this mortal existence. He ardently believed in the moral responsibility to make a society better and rejected any kind of Christian tendency to pass the buck of responsibility for life's many injustices to some vague idea of

God's mysterious purposes or to some equally vague idea of how everything will work out in the next life. He surely believed in Heaven and its justice, but I once heard him say that he imagined that even in Heaven there would be work to do and that all he hoped for when it came to salvation was the chance to give more service. He felt it foolish to wish for rewards. He knew we could make a mess of things theologically when we tried to make sense of why things happen, which is why he believed that we are on far safer terrain morally by simply accepting the responsibility to act in the face of suffering and injustice. He would often say he preferred to err on the side of mercy, presumably because he didn't want to pretend that he knew more than he did about God's justice.

My own experience with Lowell Bennion was as a camper at his Boys Ranch, which he ran for twenty-three years, in the summers of 1977 and 1978 and later as a camp counselor during the summers of 1983 and 1984, the final two summers he ran it. Which means, of course, that I knew him as "Doc," which was everyone's affectionate nickname for him there. Like many of the other boys at the ranch, I was there because he had already had an important influence on my parents who were students at the University of Utah. My brothers had already participated, and my parents wanted me to have an opportunity to learn from him. His vision for the ranch was simple: he wanted to provide boys with an opportunity to work, to work with their hands, to work with and on behalf of others. He wanted recreation too and intellectual debate, and he wanted to teach fundamental life skills. He was keen on shaping the whole boy, providing opportunities for intellectual, physical, and moral improvement. This wasn't a camp for troubled or at risk youth, except in the sense that we were all at risk, at risk of losing a relationship to our bodies, to the earth, to our minds and spirits. We needed to find purpose, discover our talents, and to find balance in life before narcissism took over. Of course, he admitted most anyone who wanted to come and that meant that some of the boys were indeed troubled and in need of special attention. Some of those boys spent more time gardening by his side than others.

He had also been a great friend to my uncle John, a man who suffered from schizophrenia, by helping him find employment and engage in service, and at one point, by taking him to Europe with his family. Our family has often marveled at his generosity toward my uncle that surely could not have been easy. A few years after I married, in the early 90s and shortly before Lowell passed away, I had the cherished chance to introduce my wife, Amy, to him. He was in the back yard working in the garden, doing work all the way to the end of his life. His body had grown infirm and his eyes had grown dim. But he was kind as ever and invited us in for some tomatoes from his garden. I was struck by the realization that he was getting close to the end and cried as we left. It was the last time I saw him.

Hardly a week goes by in my life without thinking about him and what he stood for. He has become a permanent part of my conscience. I have a picture of him in my office, weeding his garden at the ranch, to remind me of what I hope I can still become. Mormonism has produced a great many brilliant minds and, of course, an entire army of humanitarians who serve across the world, but I don't believe it has ever produced someone quite like Doc, a thoughtful and reflective sage who yoked his considerable intellectual powers to service and to the relief of suffering in his community. Unlike many intellectuals, his mind was always aimed at benefiting others, motivating them to live lives of deeper integrity, greater compassion, and more thoughtful and deliberate Christianity. And perhaps unlike many humanitarians, he was deeply committed to the life of the mind. His books were not esoteric. He wrote them for anyone and everyone, and they hewed close to the marrow of the gospel. He wanted to keep things simple, principled, and accessible, but he was also deceptively profound, helping us to see what maybe we had lost sight of. His approach to the Book of Mormon, for example, was less interested in the questions of its historicity or in its unique status in the world of Christianity but in its fundamental social ethics and concern for the poor. He helped the intellectuals of the church not to lose sight of their moral groundings, and he helped the moralists of the church to understand the importance of rethinking, revising,

and reworking our priorities so that they didn't become static and stubborn in the face of new problems.
I loved his simple formulation of priorities: people, he
would say, are the most important things in the universe and the gospel is the most effective means of
respecting, healing, and ennobling people. The church
is a best institutional setting for bringing the gospel
to people. The simplicity of his understanding gently
warned against the prioritization of institutions and
ideas over human relationships.

I devoured all of his books in my formative years
and had the great privilege of learning at his side while
weeding his garden, or doing service, or assisting him
in the work of mentoring young men at the ranch. I
don't know why he decided I might make an adequate
counselor, but in the summer of my graduation from
high school, in 1983, just six months after the tragic
death of my oldest brother from suicide and only a few
months more than that removed from a misdirected
youth, he hired me. He didn't make a big deal about my
brother's death, but he was always sure to find a moment alone with me to talk about it. He probably also
knew that the experience itself of working with saws
and hammers, working in the garden, painting widows'
houses in the valley, and hiking, fishing, and camping
with boys to help them have a meaningful experience,
were enough to heal my soul. I had lived as one of the
only Mormons in my high school in Connecticut and
had only recently become intellectually and spiritually

alive. I found myself in an embarrassment of riches, working under Doc's exceptional wisdom and inspiration and surrounded by some of the finest people my age I have ever had the privilege of knowing — Chris Cline, Brian Schmidt, Lindsay Bennion, and John Lyon—men who were passionate about ideas, committed to the values of the gospel, and dedicated to hard work, laughter, and rip-roaring outdoor adventure. And there were those young boys to attend to and mentor as well, a task I never before had the chance to do but which helped me to grow up. It didn't hurt that all of this took place in one of the most beautiful places in this country that I have ever seen, on the western edge of Teton Valley looking straight across to the exceptional peaks of the Tetons. My great life-long love of nature and concern for environmental stewardship stem from those magical summers in the Tetons that brought me needed comfort. When we weren't in his presence, we often found ourselves talking about his ideas. As we counselors worked with the boys, digging fence post holes, or skinning logs, or weeding the garden, Doc's ideas set our minds soaring, searching for ideals, and dreaming of possibilities. It was exciting to be young, to be Mormon, and to feel ourselves on the edge of truth's discovery. We felt called to a higher life, and we felt willing to respond to the call. The experience changed our lives forever. I think I speak for all of us in saying we have spent the better part of the rest of our lives trying to come to terms with and to live up to Doc's legacy.

Sadly, Doc seems virtually unknown among the younger generations of the church and his many books are all, as far as I can tell, out of print. This is despite the fact that he was the founding director of the first LDS Institute in the LDS church, at the University of Utah, and was instrumental over the course of several decades in shaping the educational culture for LDS youth, writing many books on his own as well as manuals for the church. Early on, he sensed that college-age youth in the church needed guidance in their search for understanding, especially in their quest to integrate faith and intellect. He was concerned too about the rise of selfishness in American culture and the tendency for young people to evolve into self-obsessed, narrowly focused adults who only concerned themselves about their own lives and well-being and not that of others, who pursued material well-being for its own sake, and who luxuriated in idle pursuits at the expense of the health of the larger society. He was not afraid to ask tough questions of others and even of his church leaders, some of whom were close acquaintances, whenever he saw contradiction, as he did, for example, in the church's priesthood ban for black men at the time, or when he heard people defending life at the same time that they defended capital punishment or the accumulation of nuclear weapons.

He called himself a liberal but, he liked to insist, mostly in the sense that Christ was a liberal, that is, as a selfless, generous, and freely compassionate person. In other words, while he had his political convictions, political ideology interested him not in the least. What he wanted, what he lived for, and what guided all of his thinking about society were the biblical principles of justice, mercy, and fundamental human dignity. As far as I could tell, he lived with integrity, staying true to his ideals in practice. He had his complaints and concerns about society and about the institutional church, but he had too much work to do to live up to the Christian life that he never seemed content to just sit around and complain. He always felt a need to roll up his sleeves and get to work, even serving as a Bishop very late in his life. He was a true builder. He believed that cultivating the capacity to be generous to the poor, to refrain from judging others, and to be merciful were paramount virtues of the Christian life. He worried about the tendency to place concerns for one's salvation ahead of the higher purpose of the Christian life, which is to learn to love service and selfless giving for its own sake, as the deepest and most sincere desire of the heart. The reason he liked to imagine himself in the next life working hard, quietly serving, persistently relieving suffering, and teaching was because that is who he had become and where he had found his greatest purpose and joy. When he died in 1996 after wearing himself and all of his possessions out in a very long life of service, President Gordon B. Hinckley, the President of the LDS church at the time and his former neighbor, commented at his funeral that he had seen a lot of cars in the church parking lot that day that Lowell Bennion would have never driven. He never made a show of a kind of principled vow of poverty and perhaps he never had access to enough money to live more opulently, but it just wasn't in him to own things that were unnecessarily expensive or luxurious. He believed that things were only of value to the degree that they were functional, beautiful, and well made. He was not afraid to suggest that people ought not to own homes and cars that were too big and too expensive because he knew how much these things distract us from our deeper purposes. He lived in a simple home, wore simple clothes, and was never above grabbing a garden tool or a hammer and rolling up his sleeves to do what needed to be done. He did his best teaching working side by side with others.

It was because he was a model humanitarian, a man fully devoted to higher principles of living, that his gentle and committed intellect was most impressive to me. He taught more by example than by words, so when he did teach by words, they sunk deep into the heart. I wouldn't say he was overly eloquent. He didn't relish the beauty of language for its own sake. Even his use of language stuck to his principles of being useful and beautiful and well crafted. At the conclusion of the first summer, he sent me my modest pay check, and in the envelope, he left a small note that simply said: "Keep up your lust for the fine things in life." With one simple phrase, he was reminding me not to live for my body but for my mind and spirit and for others. He was perhaps also gently encouraging what he could see was a budding passion in me for things that mattered. The truth is I was barely emerging from the fog of a poorly spent youth, one largely without discipline or direction in pursuit of my own vanity and pleasure. And I was just beginning to discover the world of ideas, of great literature and theology, to choose a purpose for my life. It was hard to find a consistent happiness in my life and hard to imagine that I could steady my own ship. He taught me I had no right to believe that the good I might do in the world, in the end, had any more to do with me than with others. We are interdependent with each other and with God, and a principled life of integrity lived on behalf of others is the only possession we can obtain in life. Everything else, it seems, is dross. So he taught me that I could, indeed, learn happiness by learning to like my life, to relish it in all its simplicity, and to care more for doing what was right than for whatever blessings, consequences, or honors it might bring me. It would take discipline and practice to learn to like life, to learn to like the best things. The good news is that the best things are simple and always available.

Here, in his words, is a brief summary of what he taught and lived by:

*Learn to like what doesn't cost much.*

*Learn to like reading, conversation, music.*

*Learn to like plain food, plain service, plain cooking.*

*Learn to like fields, trees, brooks, hiking, rowing, climbing hills.*

*Learn to like people, even though some of them may be different ... different from you.*

*Learn to like to work and enjoy the satisfaction of doing your job as well as it can be done.*

*Learn to like the song of birds, the companionship of dogs.*

*Learn to like gardening, puttering around the house, and fixing things.*

*Learn to like the sunrise and sunset, the beating of rain on the roof and windows, and the gentle fall of snow on a winter day.*

*Learn to keep your wants simple and refuse to be controlled by the likes and dislikes of others.*

All of Doc's aphorisms imply a simple principle: our goodness and happiness must begin in the heart and depend on the quality of our affections, and, perhaps most importantly, we have the capacity to change those affections through a kind of cultivation. "Learn to like," he repeats. Don't assume that what you like is unchangeable, deeply rooted in your personality like some genetic code. Our affections stem from what we serve and devote ourselves to, and even if we don't yet love as we should, it is enough to want to love better, more deeply, more generously. And loving is a way of practicing what we like. This is a hopeful teaching because it gives us a chance to change our hearts if we have the courage to begin with simple steps and learn to like more of life.

This book is simply meant to honor Lowell Bennion's legacy by reminding us of the value of these basic principles and exploring their implications for our contemporary life. It is confessional and personal. I take my own liberties in thinking about what these statements have meant in my life and might mean in our contemporary culture. My intention is to be honest in the hope that it opens up new lines of thinking and self-examination in your life. With more dramatic changes in our culture and way of life than he perhaps could have imagined, his ideas seem to me more important than ever. I revisit them in a spirit of self-examination in the hope to rekindle their relevance for today.

# Learn to like what doesn't cost much

PRICE, OF COURSE, IS NOT ALWAYS a reflection of quality, as most of us have sadly learned in this economy of increasingly poorly made products. We live in an economy that thrives on obsolescence, so durability is arguably at least one reason to buy what may cost more. Doc was not uninterested in quality. He would often repeat his mantra at the ranch about how we should evaluate things: Is it well made? Is it functional? Is it beautiful? But when he urges us to learn to like what doesn't cost much, he seems to be underscoring the importance of practicing the principles of self-restraint and frugality. The words of Paul come to mind: "But godliness with contentment is great gain. For we brought nothing into this world, and it is certain that we can carry nothing out. And having food and raiment let us be therewith content" (1 Timothy 6:6–8).

This virtue is not my strong suit. I have yet to learn the kind of contentment Paul speaks of to Timothy. Beyond food and clothing, I need (and use) a computer, a pair of bikes, a comfortable and beautiful house, heating and cooling in my cars and in my home, a smart phone, and I buy lots and lots of books. My children have had all that they need and then some. They have gone to good schools, they use computers, they have a variety of choices about their clothing, they play a family piano, a guitar, a violin, a flute, and as a family, we have five cell phones. They have bikes, iPods, soccer clothes, and running shoes. And, as someone who loves recreation, I have specialty clothes and equipment for hiking, biking, fishing, running, swimming, and tennis. I own a tandem kayak. And we all have access to the best health care in the world. I don't mean to say that I am exceedingly rich. I only mean to say that the middle-class way of life for most Americans makes me among the most wealthy the world has ever seen, by any reasonable standard.

It isn't fashionable in my profession to claim to be wealthy. Academics, especially in the humanities, like to point out how little they make, particularly in proportion to how much schooling they had to get. I spent six years in graduate school. I didn't have a salary until I was thirty. I have academic friends with Ivy League salaries and non-academic friends with less post-graduate education making a great deal more than I. So there has always been the temptation to think that life's temporal problems could be solved with more money rather than by a more modest appetite. Even if I haven't conquered my desire for material things, I learned some time ago that this kind of comparing is counterproductive. I did a lot of it when I was younger and growing up in a very wealthy community in Connecticut where, by comparison with many of my friends, I used to feel that we lived on the poor side of things.

Two years as an LDS missionary in Venezuela helped to change that. I largely spent my time with either the middle or the lower classes. Among the most poor, I found myself in neighborhoods of tin shacks, makeshift plumbing that poured down rivulets in the alleys, and makeshift wiring that stole electricity from nearby generators. Kids walked in the streets, often without clothes, like stray dogs (which were also plentiful), and because it rained often and hard and the mud splashed up the sides of houses and cars and people, everything seemed covered in dirt. I walked miles and miles every day and found myself wasting away from the sweat and exertion and from the occasional bouts with diarrhea. Slowly but surely I began to understand how distorted my understanding of wealth had been.

I started to see that not only is there a poverty of material things but there is a poverty of education and opportunity. I remember being in one particular valley in a rural town, Villa de Cura, and meeting an elderly woman who asked me where I was from. When I told her I was from the United States, she asked where that was. I said it was in the north. "Just over those mountains?" she asked. I was momentarily confused. Did she not know where my country was? Had she never heard of it? Venezuela has "estados," or states, so it occurred to me that maybe she thought I referred to a place in her country. Much farther I insisted.

It was then that I understood just how limited our mental geography is by what we know. Of course, I didn't know where Venezuela was until I received my mission call. I had to look it up in our world atlas we had at home. The poverty of imagination is, in part, a symptom of a poverty of education, and such poverty is not only ubiquitous but relative. We all need an expansion of the mind and of an understanding of the world. Travel, experience, and education are all needed to continually fill in the picture, but fuller understanding only comes in fits and starts and is never really complete. My understanding was expanding daily in Venezuela. I was grateful that my somewhat naïve and young faith had taken me far enough away from home to gain this understanding, but its culture and history were still new terrain.

Such experiences convinced me that I wanted to couple my devotion to the gospel with a devotion to education. I can say that although I am immensely happy with my career choice and believe in what I do, I am never fully convinced that what I do makes enough of a difference. I don't know how any of us could feel otherwise, no matter what we do. That woman and those streets, filled with poor children, are never far from my mind. They nag at me. They remind me that humanitarian work is needed too and much more self-restraint in my own life. I admired Doc for his devotion to the poor. Even though he was an educator and believed in and worked for the improvement of the mind, he never stopped doing work—practical service every week of his life—to improve the temporal conditions of those in greatest need. He understood that ideas were not important for their own sake, that his capacity to think rightly about things should not exceed his capacity and commitment to do good. I believe continued church service helps me to remember this.

It's because of Doc's influence that when my best friend offered me the chance to join him as a translator for a team of eye surgeons heading to the highlands of Guatemala a number of years ago, I jumped at the chance. I was just beginning my academic career, and it seemed like a way to shore up my resistance to "mission drift." I admire these men and women who give so much of their time and money and good will to bless the lives of some of the most poor in this part of the world. I have returned many times, more recently with members of my family. It never feels like enough, but it always grounds me to go. These trips remind me of my wealth. I am grateful for the financial pinch I feel to make the commitment and for the occasional realization that I will have to forgo a want because I have already spent money and time this way. Humanitarian work reminds me that even church service—which is a vital foundation for conquering the selfish tendency to surround yourself merely with those who make you most comfortable—also has its limitations in the reach it can have. The fact is our community should be much larger than the confines of what is most familiar or comfortable. Doc never limited his service to people of his own faith or to those in his own circles. His commitment was to broaden his circles however and whenever he could. I suppose the alternative is to risk believing that the world consists of people in the conditions of those most immediately around us. There is poverty in such an imagination.

There is a similar risk in believing that one experience of service is enough to teach us all what it means to be truly poor, but it is at least valuable to witness the difficulties of others, to struggle and perhaps even fail at alleviating that suffering. To have Doc's influence in my conscience leaves a nagging feeling that never really abates. It urges me to find ways to trim my otherwise opulent and wasteful lifestyle. It tells me I can always stand to remember Doc's advice. What I like about his advice is its simplicity. Doc was deeply familiar with the jeremiads of the Old Testament regarding the stranger, the fatherless, the widows, and the poor. Indeed such words were his daily bread. He was particularly fond of Micah 6:8, quoting it frequently from memory: "He hath shewed thee, o man, what is good; and what doth the Lord require of thee but to do justly, and to love mercy, and to walk humbly with thy God."

Back in the late 70s and early 80s when I knew him, less was known about the direct impact on the environment and on the quality of life of the poor that our habits of consumption had. As I think back on our conversations, I don't know that I ever had a conversation with him about environmental problems. He didn't write much about them. But he was certainly aware of the moral risks of material wants and the danger they pose to society. Today we know that we Americans consume enough that if everyone on the planet lived as we did, we would need at least four planets to feed the voracious appetites of First World living. Cutting back on our desires for consumption helps to make more resources available for others, and it helps to protect the environment. This is true not only individually but collectively. The devastating impact of our First World appetites on the poor and on the planet must not be ignored.

I recognize that I am exploring issues that go beyond the realm of price, which was Doc's original point, but it seems necessary given our contemporary circumstances. I guess it is fair to say that the principle is that we should consider what we buy and how much we spend as a moral matter. That seems especially necessary in today's global market. By definition, the free market is not a moral market. It is amoral at best and at times immoral, especially to the degree that it tries to sell what is harmful or that it champions avarice. A free market wants no regulation and has no intended direction, and yet we have treated it as if it would guide us magically and invisibly to the promised land. It simply doesn't know how to make moral choices. It doesn't want to. And it always values more and more consumption, regardless of the morality of what we consume or its impact on the earth or on others. We are so profoundly caught in the web of its ubiquity that it is fair to say that the vast majority of us who benefit most from the modern economy are the most voracious consumers in the history of the world.

You would think, then, that we Mormons would understand the urgent need to spend far more time articulating and promoting the moral principles that should guide us as consumers. Instead, we have expended more energy and time defending the free market, as if its virtue were self-evident. Indeed, we have been more fond of citing reassuringly the verse, "there is enough and to spare" from Doctrine and Covenants 104:17 than we have been of the remaining verses in the section. If we read a little more, the Lord is not so reassuring. The very next verse, verse 18, says: "Therefore, if any man shall take of the abundance which I have made, and impart not his portion, according to the law of my gospel, unto the poor and the needy, he shall, with the wicked, lift up his eyes in hell, being in torment." It seems to me that the Lord has some pretty strong feelings about the morality of our choices regarding the consumption of the earth's goods.

I don't often know what the right price for anything is—that seems part of the curse of this impersonal economy—and I don't often know what is an appropriate need and what is an inappropriate want—a curse of being human, I guess. I don't pretend, in other words, to have all the answers. I certainly know the feeling of having overspent and over-consumed, as I do the satisfaction of showing self-restraint from time to time. I suspect that not knowing and not feeling entirely comfortable are appropriate responses to being in this economy. Section 104 makes it clear that we ought to feel discomfort with the embarrassment of riches that is life in the developed world and with the persistent and nagging problem of unequal distribution of the earth's resources throughout the world. Where much is given, of course, much is expected, and certainly among those things that are expected are awareness of and compassion for the poor and a commitment to give of our surplus to relieve suffering.

But again, Doc's advice is not simply to be generous; it is to cultivate stronger contentment and a more modest appetite for things. I think he might have added that we should learn to like things that will have a lesser and kinder impact on the poor and on the earth, things like clean and renewable resources such as wind, sun, and geothermal energy, or public transportation, walking, and biking or used clothing and other second-hand materials needed for modern living. There are, of course, other renewable and renewing resources too, like the love of relationships, the experience and appreciation of beauty, and taking simple pleasure in the fundamental facts of our mortal existence. Mastercard commercials notwithstanding, there is no inherent cost to quality family time, to spending time and talking with loved ones, or to cultivating an appreciation for what is already given to us. The principle seems to be that what pleases us is a function of what we value and that the more we cultivate our imagination and powers of perception, the less likely it is that we will need material things to satisfy us. In other words, as we will see in subsequent aphorisms, Doc teaches not a kind of ascetic self-denial but rather a redefinition of pleasure and wealth.

# Learn to like reading, conversation, music

DOC WAS CONCERNED WITH how we spend our time and where our deepest affections lie. This matters not only to our character but to the communities, large and small, of which we are a part. As I suggested earlier, this is in part because how we spend our time also tends to determine how we spend our money and resources, that is, how we consume. The activities listed here—reading, engaging in conversation, and listening to or performing music—have in common the fact that they involve communing, even when done in solitude. Moreover, arguably they are not, at least not by definition, pricey or complicated activities. In ideal practice, they are activities in which we connect to a larger community or otherwise broaden our sense of the world. Because reading and conversation seem like they go better together and deserve a comparison, I will discuss first music.

For years in my home, every night I have heard piano, flute, guitar, and violin practicing in the house, the sounds of my children working on developing their musical talents. Sometimes Chopin, Beethoven, Mozart, Debussy, and sometimes popular or church songs to which my daughters liked to quietly sing. Early in his life, my son developed a passion for the guitar, and I could hear his small plying voice, exploring old Beatles classics on his not always perfectly tuned guitar. Nowadays the quality is much higher, as is the volume! I love it. Lately I hear jazz much of the time. A few years ago I was in Nashville for a conference and a friend and I made it into one of the night clubs to hear live blues music, a dream of mine. It was so loud we had to shout to make ourselves heard to one another. But the music made me so happy I wanted to cry. I couldn't explain it, but the joy of the sounds, the sheer beauty of their skilled renditions on their instruments and with their voices, made the music feel timeless. I have always found it fascinating that blues music, songs about suffering, can feel so healing. I marveled at the journey such music made over the course of the twentieth century from the neighborhoods of the most poor and underprivileged in the Deep South to a familiarity and pleasure enjoyed by the entire nation.

A number of years ago now I flew with my son to Los Angeles to visit my brother Bill, just for the chance for all of us to hear the great Gustavo Dudamel conduct the Los Angeles Symphony Orchestra in two Mahler symphonies. At the conclusion of Mahler's 2nd Symphony, one of the more extraordinary pieces of music ever composed, the choir sings words that Mahler composed himself, riffing off of lines first written by the poet Klopstock.

*What was created*

*Must perish,*

*What perished, rise again!*

*Cease from trembling!*

*Prepare yourself to live!*

*O Pain, You piercer of all things,*

*From you, I have been wrested!*

*O Death, You master of all things,*

*Now, are you conquered!*

*With wings which I have won for myself,*

*In love's fierce striving,*

*I shall soar upwards*

*To the light which no eye has penetrated!*

*Its wing that I won is expanded,*

*and I fly up.*

The performance was unlike any I had heard. Sam
was visibly shaken by the experience although he didn't
quite have the words for it. Neither did my brother
or I, although we were joined in a surfeit of emotion.
Music does this trick with thoughts, expressing them
not as ideas, at least not at first, but as sounds, and as
sounds, they are abstractions, feelings, pulses felt in the
blood. Ideas seem secondary to rhythm, to moving and
complimentary tones that must first seduce us into a

certain mood into which ideas gently drop as their setting. That is not to say that ideas do not matter or that
all of truth could be summarized as feeling. But as the
Spanish poet Miguel de Unamuno says in his marvel-
ous book, *The Tragic Sense of Life*, "the end purpose of
life is to live, not to understand" (129). Music enables
such living by reminding us of the full-bodied medium
in which language and ideas take place—in mouths
and in ears, with tongues, beating hearts and breathing lungs, flowing blood in the veins—which is why
so often we are content with beautiful but wordless
sounds. Perhaps we enjoy being relieved of the burden
of thought without being relieved of the privilege of
deeply knowing and trusting. And perhaps too it is the
pleasure of communion with others that such knowing and trusting can facilitate that we most treasure.
Music reminds us that there is no salvation without a
body, no heaven without earth, nothing more important to yearn for except that which we already have.

What are these wings that Mahler feels takes him
heavenward, these wings he has earned somehow
through the "fierce striving" of love? Why does the
wing expand, increasing his ecstasy, as he prepares to
live? And what does living truly mean? Why must one
die in order to learn to begin again, to finally, truly be
alive? Is music somehow taking us through this journey,
teaching us to die a little so we can prepare to live before
it is too late? Critics suggest that Mahler is characterized
more by his search for God than for his declaration of

having found Him. Does it signify a mere metaphor to call it, as we do, his Resurrection Symphony? Why is this striving for God so deeply moving if it is based on an agony, a striving, rather than on arrival? Why, for that matter, would the raw, off-key sounds of a boy copying popular refrains or the quiet joy of a girl at her piano feel like a kind of gritty poetry of the soul? I often wonder why I can't distinguish any longer between the joys of an old Gibson guitar and the soaring ecstasies of dozens of violins moving in unison, between the otherworldly refrains of sacred music and the earth-stained strains of unrequited love? Call me greedy, but I want all of it. Music makes me feel that I just might be so fortunate.

Reading and conversation, however, are all about words and words matter because they make dialogue and the exchange of ideas possible. Dialogue is perhaps the most important method for growing our under-standing of things and of people. Of course, neither reading nor conversation guarantees that communication happens. It all depends on our willingness and capacity to listen. Reading is a dialogue with the minds of others as long as we are not engaged in what Peter refers to as "wresting the scriptures" which can be gen-erally understood as a kind of reading that demands that the meaning of what we read or hear conforms to what we desperately, greedily, or selfishly already want the words of others to mean (see 2 Peter 3:16 and D&C 10:63). This kind of narcissism clearly cannot be what Doc has in mind. The pleasure and value of reading and conversation would seem to be the way in which these activities keep us open to others and thus curb our tendencies to treat life and others like objects or as mere reflections of ourselves. This, of course, is not what much technology today cultivates in us. Life is treated as a television or an iPhone screen where when we get bored or don't agree, with the push or swipe of a finger, we can move ourselves along to something or someone else much more to our liking. I am not suggesting modern technology is the categorical enemy. We can just as easily tune people in or out with our own attitudes and focus. But when treated with the right kind of attention that they deserve, music, reading, and conversation all require a kind of concentrated listening, a momentary emptying of the self.

I find it disturbing just how much more urgent Doc's advice seems in an age of technology that had not yet arrived when he did most of his writing. He already knew children's lives were becoming mechanized, overly structured, and selfishly focused on entertainment and pleasure. He knew too, as Wendell Berry has written more eloquently than anyone, that our bodies were rarely used any longer for work or even for recreation but were valued as commodities and determinants of self-worth. Things, of course, have only gotten worse in these regards. What happens to our relationships to ourselves, to time, to others, and what is our sense of community when we take the time to read slowly, for the sheer pleasure of it, or when we read because we are curious, thirsty for greater understanding, or simply experiencing open admiration for the chance to inhabit a gifted mind? What happens too when we take the time to really converse with someone, rather than merely exchange information? How much deeper do our conversations go, beyond the surface of brief emails, texts, or perfunctory transactions of information? True intimacy with another is becoming increasingly rare. Intimacy requires an active engagement of the imagination, profound listening, and a temporary suspension of self-interest, maybe even temporary suspension of self-awareness. A failure to truly and intimately understand the otherness of a fellow human being may be one of the most tragic failures of life. I do not believe our pursuit of Zion—becoming of one heart and one mind— will be effective without a commitment to listening to one another. True conversation certainly involves risk since it requires honesty, humility, and vulnerability. This is not unlike the risk Jesus said we must all take to lose ourselves in order to truly find ourselves again. Compassion means "to suffer with," so reading and conversation are compassion in practice, exercises in broadening and blurring the boundaries of our otherwise too narrow worlds.

It was a long time ago now, almost thirty years, but at age nineteen in 1984, I spent my last summer at Lowell Bennion's Boys Ranch as a counselor before heading off to my mission. It was also the last summer Doc would run the ranch. I had always been a social person and loved conversation. In fact, I think it is fair to say that I thrived on conversation. Much of my social life consisted of getting together with friends and talking about the big questions of life. But I was perhaps almost too extroverted. I had not yet learned to have conversations with myself, with books, or with anything other than rock music. It was as if I was terrified of being alone. I craved the company of others, and I craved stimulation, probably because I hadn't yet learned to feel vulnerable with myself, to have dialogues in my own mind. I had not yet learned that the greatest company could be my own self, my own imagination, spurred on by the words and sounds of artistic genius. I guess it was the outstanding qualities of the landscape in Teton Valley, the sincerity with which Doc treated us young counselors as his peers, and the exciting sense of possibility that conversations with Doc inspired in us about ideas, but I did something unusual with my time on my first day off that summer. Instead of listening to my cassette tapes of my favorite rock bands and writing letters to girls who kept my interest back home, I decided to spend the day at the Upper Bunkhouse reading Fyodor Dostoevsky's masterpiece novel, *The Brothers Karamazov*, which my brother had given me and had insisted I read. I was transfixed, wholly immersed in another world. I took occasional breaks and played a cassette tape recording of Beethoven's Ninth Symphony on what was called back then a boom box and stared out across the valley. I was rather proud of myself. No TV, no movie theater, no letter from a girl, nothing at all to satisfy my need for distraction. I often think now that such a day would have been inconceivable had I had a smart phone.

I look back on that day now with considerable wonder and appreciation. I was already having similar experiences with the scriptures at that point in my life, but it was my first encounter with serious literature and serious music that wasn't facilitated by a teacher, my parents, a museum, or a concert hall. I consider that day foundational to the rest of my life because I discovered, even though I was alone, that I could converse with myself, with ideas, and with feelings of an elevated sort. I had, I think for the first time, a rich inner life with which to make all future conversations, readings, and music listening all the more rich. It is a paradox, but it seems that we must guard our solitude if we are ever to expect true communion and intimacy with another human being. I must have communicated some of my budding passion for ideas to Doc because at the end of that summer, when I received my paycheck for my work, as I mentioned earlier, he wrote only one sentence on a piece of paper that was included with the check. It read: "Keep up your lust for the fine things of life." I had never heard "lust" used in relation to good things. It had never occurred to me that my rather healthy possession as a nineteen year old of passion and desire could be a gift. He helped me to see how my passions were a vital engine for life but that if they were a little more trained on the fine things of life—fine music, literature, ideas, and elevated conversation—they would bless, rather than harm, my life. I didn't have to change who I was or how I felt. I only needed to direct my attention at more elevated things. I have tried to keep follow that advice ever since.

# Learn to like plain food, plain service, plain cooking

ON THE ROAD TO EMMAUS, two men walked home. They were in deep conversation about the terrible events of the last few days. As another man joined them and asked what was on their minds, they expressed dismay that he was not aware of the news. Haven't you heard, they asked, about the great prophet who was slain and whose dead body is now missing? As the evening wore on and they arrived at home, they pled with the man to remain with them. Together they broke bread with him. Surely it was a plain meal. Nothing exceptional. Except perhaps in the way that he blessed the bread, because suddenly this ordinary and plain event of every day was transfigured into a sacrament with the Risen Lord. The men pushed away from the table and raised their arms in astonishment (at least that is how the great artist Caravaggio imagines the moment) because before them was the Savior himself.

This moving story reminds us of the holy and the exceptional qualities of the most ordinary moments of life and how easily we might miss them. It reminds us that with the eyes to see—with enough appreciation and familiarity with simplicity—ordinary food and ordinary moments become miraculous. This seems to be the impulse behind the Lord's instructions about fasting and the Sabbath Day in D&C 59:9–21. When we can put aside our distractions ("do none other thing" he says and prepare food "with a singleness of heart") we have the promise, not that the food will be the most exquisite, but that our "joy may be full." Indeed, the very "fulness of the earth shall be [ours]." I don't believe that the Lord here is promising us an opportunity for gluttonous consumption of earth's resources. Being overstuffed or glutted is not a virtue. But perhaps with more disciplined and restrained appreciation for the earth's simple gifts and for the fundamental privilege to be embodied beings on this earth, we can deepen our joy and pleasure among God's creations. His intention with the earth's bounty is not merely to feed but to "please the eye and gladden the heart... to strengthen the body and to enliven the soul." An appetite that knows no bounds can only plow through the earth and rapaciously devour its goods with a never-to-be-satisfied appetite for more. Cutting back, exercising discipline, and learning to enjoy the simple pleasures are fundamental to getting more enjoyment from less.

Doc loved gardening. He loved to share the goods from his garden. He loved weeding, almost with a kind of Zen-like contentment with the process. As he grew older, his shoulders were more stooped, his knees more naturally bent, and when I would watch him weed in his garden at the ranch, I often thought that he seemed to have worn his body into the routine crouched position of a gardener, much like the way we wear our

clothes into certain shape. I have a picture in my office
of him, crouched down, with a hoe on his shoulder, as
he reaches to pull up a weed that required the dexterity
of his bare hand. It reminds me of his closeness to the
earth, his hard work, the exhilaration he felt in laboring
with the soil. Looking at that picture, I can remember
the taste of fresh vegetables. I can remember washing
them in preparation for our meals. I remember hat-
ing but eventually learning to love a simple hot bowl
of oatmeal in the morning. Adam, we are told, was
cursed to have to bring forth food from the soil by the
sweat of his brow. Mormonism saw the Fall as a fortunate event, which means that what at first seems like
a cause for lament—bringing forth children in sorrow
and laboring with the elements of nature for our sur-
vival—are instead sources of the deepest fulfillment
and joy and perhaps even the pathway back to our
redemption. This is no small difference to see the fall
as a blessing. Suddenly the ordinary and the mundane
stand a chance of becoming the very substance of
our spiritual redemption.

Enjoying plainness and simplicity isn't just a spiritual benefit, however. It turns out that the earth is ailing
because of our voracious appetites for the next newest
thing. Once again, Doc seems ahead of his time. It
wasn't until many years later that I became more aware
of the environmental damage we have done to the
earth in the interest of an industrialized food economy.
In order to enjoy the privilege of food in all seasons,

easily accessed at our neighborhood grocery store, we have spent increasing and unsustainable amounts of energy, topsoil, and water. The average meal in America today travels 1300 miles to get to the plate. A pound of beef requires the equivalent energy of a gallon of gas to produce. If you haven't seen "Food, Inc." or "Super Size Me" or read any Michael Pollan or Barbara Kingsolver, maybe it is time. The higher up we eat on the food chain—that is, the larger and the more complex the organism (red meat being at the top)—the more energy we use in getting it to our table and the more likely it is that we have consumed unhealthy elements along the way. When you eat beef, you are also consuming the land and its biodiversity that have been cleared to grow the grain to feed the cattle, the water to feed the grain and the cattle; you are helping to destroy land habitats and drive down biodiversity; and you are helping to emit methane gas from the cattle, a very potent greenhouse gas; not to mention the fossil fuel you expend to slaughter, package, and ship the beef. Of all the body weight of all animals on earth, humans make up 30 percent and domesticated animals make up 67 percent. Only 3 percent of animals are wild. There are more pigs than people in the state of Utah. That is to say nothing about the mistreatment of animals that is the norm in the industrial meat market and that should be enough to give us pause. When we eat fast food, we are not only consuming the food and supporting the entire system of exploitation that supplies meat but also the excessive packaging that goes with it, all of it measurable in its impact on the environment and on the world's poor. If we were to reduce our meat eating by only 20 percent, according to one study, it would be the equivalent of buying a hybrid vehicle in terms of the energy we would save. Is it any wonder why the LDS practice of the Word of Wisdom advises to eat meat sparingly and to eat fruit in season? To eat food in season, one would need to conform one's diet more to the changing seasons, to eat locally, to grow more of our own food, and to cultivate the art of canning and preserves. Sure, that might mean passing up on some exotic foods like seafood if we live inland, or New Zealand lamb, or Chilean grapes. It used to be a sign of aristocratic power in the eighteenth and nineteenth centuries in England to grow and serve tropical fruits in greenhouses, as a way of showing your neighbors that your diet was free of climatic constraints. While it is no longer a sign of social power, it certainly is a sign of needless indulgence and thoughtless consumption. In our understandable urge to feed the world, we converted to larger and larger scale agriculture and more and more complex webs of trade of monocrops across the globe. So while this has led to many benefits, it has also led to an increased efficiency with which those of us in the developed world glut ourselves and degrade the earth. In America, we are increasingly overweight even as we continue to throw away uneaten food, up to 40 percent of the food we purchase. It is as if the modern food economy wanted to make aristocrats of us all, giving us the privilege of eating whatever we wanted whenever we wanted it, all at increasing cost to the climate and to the earth.

This is not without pushback, of course. We are seeing the growth of farmers' markets, community supported agriculture, a call to revive the family garden, and a new "eat local" ethos. Doc seems to be advising us to go even further and let go of our addictions to fine, elaborate, and exotic foods prepared by others. He wants to bring food production and preparation back into a more simple and home-based economy. In this sense, "plain" does not have to imply plain tasting. I at least hope not. I can't speak for Doc's taste in food, but fresh and homemade food is generally tastier in any case. Everyone knows how much better a garden tomato tastes than one bought in the store, especially one bought out of season. As we become adults, many of us instinctively yearn for the taste of fresh food and for the chance to recover the art of cooking from scratch. This is despite the fact that children are often disgusted with the sights and smells and textures of foods that are not processed, packaged, and artificially flavored. We can see here in all of Doc's aphorisms a mandate to recover our autonomy and creativity and embrace direct responsibility for how we consume.

It is not what goes in us, Jesus taught, that corrupts us but what comes out of the heart. Diet is a moral matter not just because certain things are good for us and certain things are bad or even because what we eat directly affects the temple of the body or because it directly takes from the sacred body of the earth. Eating is a moral matter because it is an inherently violent act. That is nothing to be ashamed of if we do so reverently, or as the 59th section of the Doctrine and Covenants cited earlier describes it, with a "singleness of heart." Violence that is witnessed, accounted for and consecrated is what we call sacrifice. If we eat without lust, without gluttony, but with purpose and gratitude and recognition of the sacrifice of labor, of land and resources that have been laid upon the altar, we make a sanctified meal, a sacrament, possible. This phrase from section 59 comes in the context of the Lord's teaching on the fast. If we deny ourselves of food for spiritual purpose and for a designated time, this simple act of restraint can help us return to the act of consumption with a more reverent and sanctified attitude of appreciation for the gift of life. The law of chastity is not a law that sees sexual intimacy as a degrading thing. It is holy, and precisely for that reason, it merits self-control and proper context. In the same way, the law of the fast teaches renewed appreciation for the gift of physical life, physical pleasure, and the spiritual benefit of earthly nourishment. Eating is violent but it can be holy. It can be redeemed by the proper frame of mind and a body devoted to service.

I admit this has been a struggle for me. I am sure I am not alone, but that does not give me any comfort.

It has been a long struggle to learn to eat more sensibly and with more thought. It is easy to slip into a state of unthinking response and treat food as a pill to give me energy, to eat to relieve stress, or to neglect the importance of savoring what I eat. Like many people, I have had to work hard to avoid eating more than I should and to eat a healthy diet. I try to pray in true gratitude for my food, but it easy to treat such a prayer as a shallow ritual. I wish I were a better cook and a better gardener, but I am determined to improve. I am grateful for how fasting teaches me to repent. I am grateful that my wife insisted a long time ago on the priority of sitting down nightly to a healthy dinner as a family. It gives us time to talk, to revisit the day, to laugh and enjoy each other, and to enjoy recipes that we will remember for the rest of our lives. After I spent six months living in Germany as a student, I came to appreciate the beauty of a beautiful breakfast spread and taking the time to eat slowly, talk of the news and of life, and to increase bonds of affection one with another. We Americans, I could see by contrast, are opportunistic eaters, rarely taking the time to treat eating as a simple and social act.

I don't suppose Doc ever cared much for eating out, so I suppose he would want us to stop going out so often. He does seem to imply the value of the hard work it takes to establish our own food independence. I don't think, however, that such independence comes from storage, at least not exclusively. In our drive to store food for emergencies, we would do well to re-member that food safety is more sustainably and meaningfully secured with greater levels of household production and support for gardening and local agri-culture than by mere storage.

For those of us who love fine cuisine and savor-ing the cuisines of the world, Doc's advice might be a tough sell. The good news is that many restaurants and many cooks in the home have caught the vision of the value of local, fresh, and organic produce, however. In all cases, we must also consider what we give up when we pay others to feed us. This includes the time to build relationships at home, to develop discipline, independence, and creativity, and the opportunity to bring ourselves in closer contact with and to be better stewards over the local ecosystems that support us.

I don't know if by "plain service" Doc meant service of food alone, as we might conclude by in-cluding service in this list, but since he was a devout practitioner of humanitarian service which included but was not limited to the sharing of good food, per-haps we can imagine it simply means that we should focus on the simple pleasures of giving simply, rather than worrying ourselves so much about dramatic out-comes or effects of our service. To like "plain ser-vice" might mean to learn to give our attention to the most obvious and immediate needs of others. We shouldn't, in other words, overthink service. We sometimes put too much pressure on ourselves and imagine that dramatic results must ensue. I like the Jesuit principle of meeting people where they are at and seeking to identify what the next simple step might be that they need to take in their lives. We don't have to solve all problems at once. We only need to be present for those who are in our immediate surroundings and get to know them and their needs. Too often we forsake the chance to make our humble offerings to others because we imagine that our acts of giving are not particularly creative, elegant, or impressive or that they need to have a larger impact. And in thinking more about ourselves or about the effects of what we give, we not only bypass the chance to meet simple needs, we fail in the basic quest of service to forget ourselves and love others. How ironic it would be if a self-conscious and vain attitude about selfless service would obstruct our ability to give at all. Service, in other words, should not be merely intended to affect change but also to change relationships. What we should give, in all cases, is ourselves—our presence, our time, our attention—not some substitute. That is not to say that many people don't need specific things—food, clothing, shelter, for starters—it is merely to say that receiving material gifts means more when we are also receiving a relationship, a bond, an opportunity to escape the solitude of *all* forms of destitution: material, spiritual, *and* emotional. The "substance" that King Benjamin asks us to impart (see Mosiah 4:26), in other words, is all that we are—our story, our emotions, the way we see the world, how we think, as well as what we have, what we have learned, and what we know. In this sense, everyone has wealth to share.

# Learn to like fields, trees, brooks, hiking, rowing, climbing hills

THIS MIGHT HAVE THE APPEARANCE as one of the most comfortable aphorisms of Doc's, since appreciation of this sort would appear easy to come by. I have never met a person who did not have at least a modicum of respect for natural beauty of some kind. I have listened to grown men weep about the feelings of intimacy they have felt with the Creator on a mountainside during a deer hunt. I know biologists and zoologists who feel purely at home among the insects and animals of the wild. And in all my years of growing up and then serving in youth programs in the church, I have witnessed the calming and healing effects of the outdoors on anxious souls. People are starved for nature and they will spend incredible amounts of money to travel to some of the most beautiful landscapes on earth. Many of them, of course, come to my home state to enjoy the red rock wonders of southern Utah.

What amazes me, however, is how poorly we have understood our relationship to nature, how shallowly we love it, and why we continue to make the mistake of assuming that nature is something "out there" or even far away and not in the very substances of our bodies, our homes, our clothing, our food, and our modes of transportation and indeed in our own neighborhoods. We love nature but our way of life is destroying it, even our way of loving it. Indeed, despite an almost universal instinct for love of nature, it is a rare human soul who feels awakened to its destruction and feels called to act on its behalf. Fierce affection for nature without due attention to its health and flourishing is another way of treating nature as a commodity or thing to be possessed and used but then discarded. Affection without ethical care for the health of nature is akin to pornographic desire because it is more interested in gratification than service and sanctification.

That is merely to say that Doc holds us to a much higher standard than we might at first think. The truth is, it hasn't exactly been easy over the course of human history to find beauty in ordinary nature. One look at the history of art is sufficient to realize that it wasn't at least until the Renaissance that we began to see images of somewhat ordinary landscapes in paintings and as late as the early nineteenth century when we saw them finally unadorned by the whimsical imaginations of the artist or by the weight of mythology and history that art critics demanded of landscape paintings. In their long battle for supremacy with the poets, painters had convinced themselves that painting wasn't a high art unless it was philosophy and it wasn't philosophy if it didn't embellish on reality. We spent the better part of

Western history, in other words, believing that nature needed enhancement to be beautiful. And this had no small influence on our modern tendency to believe that nature isn't truly beautiful until we have developed it for human use, even if such development changes it beyond recognition or damages its ecological health. But to the degree that we began in earnest to let go of these pretensions, we found we were scarcely up to the task. The Impressionists alone are proof that reality is inexhaustible and inexhaustibly beautiful. We now know, or at least we should, that we are always playing catch up to the wonder of this world.

Woody Allen, no nature lover, was fond of saying, "Nature and I are two." Which reminds me of another joke I once heard on the old radio show, "Car Talk":

"What did the Buddhist monk say to the Hot Dog vendor?"

"Make me one with everything."

These jokes bring into focus a more serious point. We are neither entirely apart from or exactly the same as the physical environment that surrounds us. Biologically, we are indeed one and maybe at times we can feel inklings of a kind of belonging to the universe that feels as if our consciousness dissolves, but our consciousness never dies entirely, nor should it. It is one of our greatest gifts—this capacity to ponder, consider, reflect, analyze and self-formulate. This innermost sense of being separates us from the world, even at the very moments when we feel conjoined; consciousness feels eternal and linked to God and is at the root of our agency and our capacity for growth and understanding. The paradox is that we could scarcely experience wonder at the universe at all if it were not for our human capacity for conscious self-reflection. We need, in other words, our human difference *in order to imagine our kinship with the Creation.*

I suppose it is obvious that I am interested in something more than what it means to love camping in the outdoors. Some do, some don't. Some of us love the feel of sweat running down our back as we ascend a trail or even relish the sensation of a warming body as it exercises in the cold, frigid air of winter. Some of us prefer our bodies to remain in a permanent state of 70 degrees comfort and generally cringe at the thought of going more than a day without a shower. I would argue for the value of experiencing the senses in their full range, if for no other reason than to remind us of our bodies, which can become almost invisible to us in a modern world that has essentially rendered them useless. And the best way to become aware of our bodies is to engage the senses outdoors. As it is, we only seem to notice our senses when they stop working like they should. So, yes, I feel a certain pity for people who don't know the vicissitudes and pleasures of a body exposed to the world in the more vulnerable way afforded by being in the outdoors. When I see folks walking on treadmills on a perfectly beautiful day, I wonder.

But it is a fair question to ask: must we *love* nature? Isn't it enough to respect it? Isn't there a risk of loving nature more than human beings? Isn't that a kind of idolatry? All fair questions, as I say. I like President Joseph F. Smith's answer best: "We have eyes and see not, for that which we cannot appreciate or admire we are largely blind to, no matter how beautiful or inspiring it may be. As children of God, it is our duty to appreciate and worship Him in His creations. If we would associate all that is truly good and beautiful in life with thoughts of Him, we would be able to trace His handiwork throughout all nature" (Kelson 24). In other words, what matters, I think, is how well we understand nature as a gift. As we read in D&C 59:

> *18 Yea, all things which come of the earth, in the season thereof, are made for the benefit and the use of man, both to please the eye and to gladden the heart;*
>
> *19 Yea, for food and for raiment, for taste and for smell, to strengthen the body and to enliven the soul.*
>
> *20 And it pleaseth God that he hath given all these things unto man; for unto this end were they made to be used, with judgment, not to excess, neither by extortion.*

It makes little sense to claim that we love and worship God if we cannot love and worship him *in his creations*, the gifts of physical life that are the very manifestations of his love made flesh. If we claim that we are grateful for our lives, we ought to include in our consideration the very web of life and the biological processes that make our physical life possible and the divine love that sustains our capacity to move and have our being in a fragile world. Although spiritual beings, we find ourselves earth-bound, bounded by bodies, stuck in plasma and circulating blood, breathing, moving, touching the world and each other at every turn. We see, feel, hear, smell, and taste the world and each other. This also means that we feel both pain and joy, we know suffering and relief, and we can experience health as well as sickness. Ultimately we die even as we come to yearn for and understand the gift of eternal life. The world and its many others are known to us through the senses, just as we are known to ourselves. This is not to say, of course, that all that we know only comes through the senses—there is, of course, the spiritual means of knowing—but, as the scripture above teaches, it is scarcely possible to begin to apprehend what stands above and apart from physical experience without being fully immersed in it. If the emphasis on an embodied God and an embodied and earth-bound heavenly destiny in Mormon theology should teach us anything, it is that we ought not to be in a rush to leave or denigrate the miraculous experience of embodiment nor to see it as something separate from the spirit.

But I also understand that we are not all of the same disposition. I would like to do away with the stereotype of the nature lover, the tree hugger, the outdoor fanatic. This is not what is required of love.

Just as I would like to do away with the stereotype that loving nature is sufficiently expressed by taking a few moments to admire a beautiful sunset or a landscape painting. If we consider what Christ said about love, the task is much steeper and more challenging. Hopefully a law of higher morality has taught us that love is superficial, even dangerous, when it loves an object, when it loves superficial or temporary beauty, when it seeks to possess and control, when it loves selfishly and willfully. Nature is a great test of our own narcissism. If we learn to love nature, or to paraphrase President Smith, to worship God in his creations, to see life as his gift, then we have to stretch the mind wide enough to imagine that all of it—every twig lashing the eye, every storm wreaking havoc, every unexpected and even unwanted change in the weather, and yes, all beautiful sunsets and all fantastical and wondrous species—all of this is part of the great expansive experiment that is our human life. And we can no more afford to be dismissive or willfully ignore the ugly and deeply troubling aspects of the creation than we can ignore the inherent weaknesses in our own flesh. Just as we must learn to consecrate our experiences, to live with sufficient faith that God can and will transform our darkest experiences into something for our own good, we must learn to see all of nature, to welcome all of its unpredictability, its harshness, its ugliness, its oppositions. To paraphrase Rilke, we must imagine a time when we can see that our nights of sorrow have been transformed into the dark green meaning of our lives. To love nature is to love mortality, to accept, even embrace, the paradoxes of our human condition, and to live in great hope not despite but because of the oppositions we experience. This is love with staying power. This is love that will not lash out in vengeful fits of anger, as we so often do to others and to a world that refuse to conform to our wishes. This is Christ's love. Which only makes sense, since it is his world, after all, a world he not only created but also suffered . . . for us.

Doc is not describing exotic locales, the likes of which we might see on a cruise or an excursion, but the simple and mundane places that most immediately surround us. If you have seen the film, "The Tree of Life," then you know what kind of deeper perception of beauty is required in order to imagine that the trees of one's childhood—in the case of the film the trees of Waco, Texas—could be seen as the trees of eternal life, or at least as portals into heaven. The film so lovingly passes through, by, and underneath these trees while sacred music plays, one feels that it is a wonder that we don't all drop what we are doing and stare. One telling phrase from the LDS account of the creation should haunt us: "And out of the ground made I, the Lord God, to grow every tree, naturally, that is pleasant to the sight of man; *and man could behold it*. And it became also a living soul" (Moses 3:9). Aesthetic value is primary here. Sure, we are told that Adam and Eve discover that trees are useful for food, for fuel, and for shelter (and we now know they are central players in the regulation of our delicate climate), but they are first and foremost something wonderful to behold. This is their gift and our privilege. True too, of course, of the fields and brooks of which Doc speaks. Elegant in their simplicity, strange in their familiarity, spiritual in their physicality, the earth and its many forms challenge us to find language, culture, and lifeways adequate to the mystery of what it means to be alive in the body.

Marilynne Robinson is one of our greatest living novelists and she is also one of America's most important Christian thinkers. If you are familiar with her fiction, you know that the landscape is almost a protagonist in the worlds she depicts and it is a site of intense possibility and yearning for her characters. In 2004, a colleague and I had the privilege to interview her, and we asked about this relationship between people and their home landscapes. This is what she said:

> *It seems to me as if every local landscape is a version of the cosmic mystery, that it is very strange that we're here, and that it is very strange that we are what we are. In a certain sense the mystery of the physical reality of the human being is expressed in any individual case by the mystery of a present landscape. The landscape is ours in the sense that it is the landscape that we query. So, we're created in the fact of ourselves answering to a particular sense of amazement. . . . One of the ways that they have of hiding from human*

> *reality is to create artificial environments. Look at*
> *people from Babylon forward; when people have power*
> *they create an artificial environment around them-*
> *selves that can suggest to them that they're immune*
> *from the consequences of being mortal. And palaces,*
> *all these things, are monuments to this impulse. . . . to*
> *the point [now] that we have no idea where we are by*
> *looking at what surrounds us.* (114)

I have given this passage much thought. I am still amazed that it came out of her on the spot. It was obvious she had given it much consideration over the course of her life. She is influenced by the theology of Calvin who believed that the natural world was a shimmering garment that both concealed but at times revealed the glory of God. For her, therefore, it is a Christian duty to pay close attention to God's creations. And what is significant, I think, is how ennobling and sanctifying awe and wonder are. She goes so far as to say that we are "created" in the act of "answering to a particular sense of amazement." This astonishment, in other words, is what makes us human, tempting an-other theologian, William Brown, to posit the idea that maybe what distinguishes us as a species isn't so much our capacity for knowledge ("homo sapiens" or know-ing man) but our capacity for wonder ("homo admi-rans" or wondering man) (4).

If no success can compensate for failure in the home, I am tempted to say that neither can any success in our man-made lives compensate for a failure to be amazed at what lies outdoors. Why is this? Just ask Job. For one thing, such amazement places us in proper perspective and helps to heal our human wounds and tame our egotism. Why else would the Lord have answered Job's pleas for comfort and release from his sorrows with an extended lecture on biology and astronomy? Why else would the Lord ask us to return to the temple often only to make us confront, over and over again, the story of the Creation. In his vision, Moses learned two vital facts about us: we are spirit children of loving parents and we are in the midst of a creation of such immensity and grandeur and beauty that we are also "nothing" in comparison. When he says that he now knows man is nothing, I don't think he means we are insignificant. To experience our own nothingness, as King Benjamin reminds us, can be helpful in putting our lives in proper perspective in the face of creation. In all our doing and making and creating, we must not lose sight of the fact that we are created beings who haven't earned this gift of life. Why else would he call us "unworthy creatures" (Mosiah 4:11)? Once we understand ourselves as interdependent not only with each other but with all of life, as part of something much grander, much more complex and vast and diverse than our puny human interests, we begin to comprehend how strange and unnecessary beauty really is, as strange and as unnecessary as love or grace or forgiveness and mercy. And when we see them unnecessary but nevertheless real, we see them as gifts of a Giver. Such awareness most meaningfully begins in a home landscape.

The older I get, the less I understand the meaning of natural beauty, even though it is also true that I more desperately depend on it than ever. I think it used to mean that the world was friendly, that if I could capture a beautiful sunset or the angle of the sun illuminating the leaves of a tree, that somehow I had found meaning and grace because I was known by someone, somewhere. But as I have gotten older, beauty causes a heartbreaking alchemy of sadness and ecstasy, as if beauty always demands an acceptance that joy and woe are indistinguishable. Because beauty feels lonely to me, so stealthy that it scarcely seems probable. And yet there it is, standing with a kind of nakedness before all the world, and all you can catch is a glimpse, for a brief moment, before it departs quietly into the folds of existence. It does still feel like love but somehow never deserved and certainly more meaningful if it is not greedily sought or selfishly expected.

A few years ago in October I took a horseback riding trip into the Sawtooth Wilderness with two of my closest friends from my college days, Keith and Andy. We were all approaching the half century mark and we hadn't all three been together for many, many years. So it was good to rekindle our friendship and to return to our more adolescent sense of humor. Not surprisingly, neither task was hard to do. We had spent the better part of the morning hours packing Keith's horses into the trailer and preparing all of the equipment, driving to the trailhead not far out of Stanley, and then climbing our way up to about 10,000 feet through some spectacular alpine wilderness after a brief cold front had swept through and left a dusting of snow among the fallen trees and on the boulder fields we passed. Our destiny was a high mountain lake where we hoped to fish with our float tubes that we packed on the backs of the horses.

After several hours, we passed across a talus of large boulders sloping steeply downward to our left below jagged cliffs to our right. The horses crossed with great caution. My horse, new to high mountain trails, was especially nervous, and before I knew it, I felt him give way beneath me, losing his footing and dropping to his chest, over-correcting and taking his hind legs off the edge of the trail on the downhill side, and then finally correcting again by swinging me into the rocks on the upper side of the trail where he pinned me against the flat face of a rock. I felt that this was my chance to bail, so I slipped out of the saddle, just barely getting my last foot out of the stirrups as the horse found his footing again and stood up and bolted away. I could tell that if not for the smooth face of the rock, I would have broken my femur or perhaps my hip, and that if not for the horse's escape from the slip downhill, it might have been worse. But I didn't yet know how much damage the fall had done to me.

Andy is a doctor, so I was lucky to have him there immediately to check me for any signs of serious injury.
Eventually I stood and could feel what later proved to
be large bruises on my right hip and on the inside of
my calf, the latter which later became a large hema-
toma. But I was okay. Shaken, and still in shock about
what almost happened, I walked the horse for a while
so that both of us could regain our confidence. But it
was literally back in the saddle again. I knew I had to
get back on. I did, and after another hour of climbing, we finally arrived at the lake. I was so glad to be
off of the horse, even though I still knew I had to get
back on and ride several hours back out to our truck.
We laughed about it and described to each other what
we had seen and experienced in those few seconds of
uncertainty. And as we opened our food, Keith offered to pray and bless the food. As he thanked God
that I was okay, we all felt an overwhelming sense of
gratitude. Later, when I finally got into my waders and
found my way out into the middle of the beautiful lake,
I prayed and the gratitude amplified. It wasn't just my
safety for which I felt grateful, which of course was
no small thing, but something else came over me. The
water was still and the lake was glass. It was a deep aqua
blue, the sky was clear, and the jagged peaks surround-
ing us were whited by the recently fallen snow. The air
was crisp, nippy, threatening in its temporary abeyance
in the afternoon warmth before what surely would be a
very cold night. I floated on the water, without any real

interest in fishing, although I casted repeatedly into the water and moved around as if I were. I was in a state of stupefaction, feeling the uncanny possibility that I would be alive at all and that this stunning beauty could be observable by anyone. I thought that if I were to die and I had any kind of feeling for nostalgia for this earth, surely this would be a logical place to want to revisit. I imagined the thousands of people who had seen this lake over the many centuries of human occupation in this corner of the world. Would they not haunt these mountains just as much as they might haunt their former homes? Assuming most of those homes were long since destroyed for the vast majority, would this not be a preferred place to come to remember their brief and odd pilgrimage on this earth? Who could expect that heaven would offer anything more beautiful than this? Who would not miss this? And why was I, so contingent, so fragile, so insignificant in this vast universe, here in this moment seeing what I was seeing? Why was this particular set of geological and atmospheric circumstances so aligned through deep and shallow time alike, conspiring together to allow this particular expression of grace? Why should I assume that I might just as easily lose my life or lose the chance to see beauty as I am to live and to experience it? We are time bound, weather bound, standing in the shallows of time, while all around us deep processes continue, molding the shape of things, of mountains and clouds alike, and making both death and beauty equally possible. Wallace Stevens was right: death is the mother of beauty. So I can't help feeling that to experience beauty is to die just a little bit. I don't say this to sound morbid. Quite the opposite. Coming into contact with the mortality and temporality of all things strangely makes life taste all the sweeter.

A word about recreation is needed here too. Doc doesn't mention ATVs, boats, or cruise ships. He had lived to see the explosion of interest in recreation that began after World War II and that hasn't stopped in its many commercialized advancements. We are all seeking our paradise on earth, only now instead of working for it, we want to buy it or mechanize our relationship to it. Fifty years ago the average visit to the Grand Canyon was two weeks. Now it is closer to two hours. As I intended to thematize in *Home Waters*, recreation and affection for nature are no panacea for the environmental problems we face. As Wallace Stegner made clear, we can love a place and still be dangerous to it, and this is due in no small measure to our method of relying on wasteful technologies instead of on our own bodies. (It doesn't help that we now know too that the small engines that propel most recreational machines are exponentially more wasteful and damaging to the environment than larger engines, making an hour of use in many cases the equivalent of using a full tank of gas in an automobile.) Yet again Doc suggests that we would do well if we could learn to simplify the way we enjoy nature. Being physically present in it—walking, hiking, rowing—makes our bodies work to earn our reward of coming closer to the earth's allure and teaches us something of the rhythms of a place.

In the end, superficial exposure to nature, as if at a diorama, doesn't captivate us enough to change our rushed and mechanized lives and inspire better care of the world. I don't mean to sound redundant, but it was at Doc's Boys Ranch in Teton Valley at the age of twelve when I really entered my embodied existence and discovered the value of physical work and of physical recreation. I discovered that the gift of embodiment, the gracious gift of life itself, gave me the unique privilege and responsibility to serve, build, care for, and experience the world. Not much else seemed to matter, and not much else matters still.

# Learn to like people, even though some of them may be different ... different from you

THE FACT IS THAT ALL PEOPLE are different and different from you. So Doc is in essence warning us not to forget this important fact. Jesus was intent on teaching us the dangers of narcissistic love—the kind of love that only flourishes among and for those who love us, that only persists in the context of requited affection, even the kind of love that worships a God fashioned after an image of ourselves and of our own predilections and preferences. We are willful beings and easily blinded by desire. We could spend an entire marriage loving a different person than the one we married simply because we never really knew or understood who they really are or because we simply failed to see their crucial differences. We could spend an entire life loving an *idea* of God, rather than the true and living God. The scriptures emphasize the importance of falling into the hands of a "living" God, which I suppose means that he is capable of communication and relationship but only if we are open to his difference and newness and willing to be changed by entering into a relationship with him.

The hitch, of course, is that all lovers will insist that by all means they love and they love truly and devotedly and that therefore it would be sacrilege to raise doubts about their object of devotion. The overly confident lover is blind to the potentially self-serving nature of affection, to the possibility that he himself is the object of his affections. For this reason, Jesus taught that the true test of love was how we might speak and think of our enemy, what resentment or fear or narcissistic need we might harbor in order to sustain the illusion that our enemy must be hated. No, he says, he must be loved and loved as purely and persistently as you love yourself or as you love those most like you, or those who love you the most.

This is really almost absurd when you think about it. I love my mother and my father and my brother irrationally. I say that because somewhere deep inside I know that they aren't in any rational sense the *best* mother or the *best* father or the *best* brother. They certainly don't believe that they are. But that's how I think of them. And I believe it when I say it. And I tell my wife she is the most beautiful, the most intelligent, the strongest woman I know. I love my kids beyond reason altogether. They are precious beyond words. Does any of this love really make any sense? Do I know any woman as well as I know my wife? Of course not. So why should I love her preferentially, with so much bias and inordinate affection? Were my children really the cutest babies, the most important children in my community?

I treated them as if they were. And you would question my love for my children if I didn't. But Jesus said if I really loved him, I would be willing to forsake them all. What?! What kind of God is he?! Why is he asking me to sacrifice affection on the altar of charity? What kind of joy is possible when even in your deepest attachments you must learn a generic love that remains steady and the same for all? Why must deep affection slowly and inevitably make room for charity, for pure love that demands nothing whatsoever from the object of love and that, in the end, cannot be any greater or any less for any one person? Is not that a world without respect of persons, without preference, a world without passion? How can love be meaningful otherwise?

I don't know all the answers, but something does happen to you as you age and as you struggle to love in a family. You are more familiar with each other's weaknesses and more familiar with your own weaknesses. And over time you can see the possessive and selfish nature of your affections. You know this in part because you discover that those affections can abandon you much too easily when things don't go well. In those moments, your affections seem totally disconnected from the person you thought you loved and more a product of your own wishes and dreams. You can lash out in anger or retreat in hurt but perhaps you look upon your relationships and for a moment you can't even imagine what will sustain you through the next week. But the week comes and goes. And so does another. And life moves on. And at some point you know you must recover those feelings if there is any chance for happiness to return again to your life. So you dig deeper into commitment and hard work and prayer and, slowly or suddenly, affection returns. This is when you discover that affection is not some disease you catch from the proverbial cherub's arrow. It is not something you can't control. You don't choose your affections exactly but they are a function of your psychology and personality, so you need to own up to them somehow. And in so doing, you can educate them, refine them, refurbish them with more noble and selfless desires, redeem them with deeper repentance and more heartfelt pleas to God for charity in rough waters. And when the affections return and couple themselves to a purer and more sustainable love, you begin to realize that you are loving your spouse, your children, and your other loved ones just a little bit more as God loves them. Somehow he loves them as they are and even though this love is available to everyone, it never feels generic and it is always rooted in the peculiar and rare and even exceptional person that is every child of God.

Armed with this understanding, you are now prepared to venture out and love those different from you. God commands you to love the stranger. He commands you to be kind to the least among you. He tells you that they—more so even than the loved ones you hold so close—are the true test of your love for

Him. It is in their face that we should see the Savior. Not at the expense of family and friends, of course, but as an extension of the bonds of family and kin, as a perpetual act of adoption, making of others new brothers and sisters even without the benefits or challenges of blood relation. We are to be in the business of building a retrofitted model of the nuclear family so as to include the entirety of the human family. Ordinary people, or especially extraordinarily different people—these are the true tests of our capacity for love. Because if we can't see God in the countenances of the most strange, the most different, then we don't really understand the meaning of his love.

A famous British atheist biologist once said that if there is a God, he is inordinately fond of beetles. In a world of over 300,000 species, he had a point. I think this statement is worth further reflection, especially in relationship to people. There is a God. And apparently he does like beetles. He also likes ants and dinosaurs, microbes and bacteria. Deserts, mountains, plains, rivers, and volcanoes. Those too. The deep ocean. And surely he likes clouds. Not to mention lots and lots of people. He likes Americans, Ecuadorians, Jews, Hindus, gypsies, and Turks. He likes the Chinese and he likes the Andorrans. He likes men and women, children and the elderly, liberals and conservatives, people of all shapes and sizes. We learn something about God just by empirically observing and absorbing the world. And when we remember that God created all of it, that he pronounced all of it good, then perhaps we gain a deeper appreciation for what his love means. We all live with mental images of the world that tell us what is normal and more or less what to expect. And yet that mental geography we carry in our minds is woefully inadequate to the world's diversity of life and peoples and cultures and individuals. Any time you travel or venture into learning about another culture or language or religion, you find yourself lost in a complex world with a deep history of difference that is almost inconceivable and certainly more than enough for a lifetime to master. The same is true when you really get to know someone from an entirely different walk of life. And the first reaction is sometimes to doubt that we all truly belong to the same family.

I remember a small crisis of faith on my mission instigated by an encounter with difference that was previously inconceivable to me. It happened the very first week. I was converted to the gospel. I was eager to teach, but I was terrified by the strange feeling of the streets of Venezuela, by the language I couldn't yet penetrate, and by the sights and smells and shape of the place. On our first day, we were let into an elderly and poor woman's home. She was not particularly excited by our presence, that much I could tell, but my companion was eager to show me how a discussion worked. As my companion projected a slide of the First Vision on the wall in her home, a small lizard walked across the image of the Joseph Smith kneeling in the sacred

grove. Suddenly I thought to myself: "What am I doing
here? Why am I so far from home? Can the story of
the gospel really extend this far in its relevance? This
woman doesn't even care about this." I was becoming
aware of my cultural bias, my narrow world that I had
been raised in, but instead of doubting the adequacy
of my worldview, I instead doubted God. I wrestled
with this feeling for several days, eventually coming to
understand how irrational my doubt was. Did I really
think that God was unaware of the world I had entered? That he didn't know and love each person I met
as much as he did me? Why was I so willing to shrink
His vision when it was mine that needed to expand?
God is our father and his love extends to all. So he
apparently loves an enormous number of people who
know absolutely nothing about the restored gospel, let
alone about my middle class American life. Most of
them don't speak English. The vast majority of them
are not white. It's a safe bet that 50 percent are women.
Many are very old. Many are so young they don't yet
know how to speak. Over a billion of them don't have
access to clean drinking water and live in extreme poverty. And most have suffered far more than I will ever
know. I needed to get over myself.

I remember Senator Bill Bradley saying a generation
ago about racial tension in America that if you didn't
have a friend of a different race, you were part of the
problem. I liked the straightforward simplicity of his
argument. We associate too often with people who are

like us and not enough with people who challenge our assumptions. I think that still holds today not only for race but for tensions between liberals and conservatives, between the rich and the poor, immigrants and citizens, religionists and secularists, town and gown, and so on. I remember the way my fellow students at Berkeley used to talk about Republicans back in the 90s. I finally had to ask them if they actually knew any Republicans, because it seemed they were describing a cartoon character. I feel the same way when I hear how liberals are described by conservatives who have been bitten a bit too hard by the right wing bug. Our choices become less meaningful when they are too few and too predictable. Genuine choice is threatened by staid tradition, chauvinism, censorship, and intimidation. Consensus that relies on habitual and categorical trust of some and distrust of others is a threat to the free flow of information and to freedom itself. Is it too bold to say that freedom *depends* on diversity?

Isaiah reminds us that "more are the children of the desolate than the children of the married wife" (Isaiah 54:1). In the end, family—the traditional family of a father, a mother, and children—will be and already is increasingly rare. But this is no excuse for retreat into self-pity or for self-congratulatory narratives we tell ourselves about how our goodness stands up against a sea of wickedness. These are not people to be discarded. The growing numbers of those who wander and are broken off from society, from the structure of family, from the joys and pleasures of stable and loving family relationships—they represent an increased opportunity and challenge to "learn to like" them. Sure, they are different. What did you expect? Sure, they dress and eat and speak and socialize differently; they believe and act differently too. Should we demand or at least urge upon them a change of habit so that they conform more to our patterns of life? Surely it is not a bad thing to teach someone who is in sin what might bring them greater happiness. Surely not, but just as surely, Jesus tells us, it is a bad thing to teach the truth without true love. And the only way to know for sure is if you have that sustaining love is when the differences remain and you find a way to keep on striving in love. This might seem like a curse. Must I love someone who is not interesting, strange, and completely unlike anything I have ever encountered before? Must I love this person who is no true friend of mine? This person who rejected me? Must I forgive this person who has harmed me and continues to pose a threat to me? No one need put themselves in harm's way. This is not what Christ is asking. But when we take needed steps of self-defense, it remains at least spiritually harmful to retreat and seek physical safety while harboring deep hatred and anger. Those are wounds we will take with us and perpetuate on our own fragile selves until we can learn charity—charity for them, but charity for ourselves too. Even the differences inside of us, the negativity and the struggles, the dark weaknesses that we work so hard to hide from others—these too must be loved, accepted, longsuffered in true charity. Why? What happens to those differences when we love in this way? Do we have to pretend they aren't there? Do we have to see them as categorical positives? What if the differences are disturbing?

I think we need to love as God loves because it helps us to shed what understandings of the world are merely a product of our own moment and place in a culture and that have nothing at all to do with the gospel. We can't see our biases and blindspots until we learn to listen to others. We can't escape them entirely, but we can begin to understand our profound need for relationships with all kinds of people. In this way, we also begin to catch a better glimpse of the nature of our Father in Heaven. Many of those differences, if not most, might prove in the end to be superficial, or conversely they might turn out to be utterly important and worth cherishing. If we can convert our weaknesses into strengths through the healing powers of the atonement and thereby learn that our weaknesses can become our allies, so too can our enemies teach us a great deal about your own follies and illusions. In the process, they might even become friends. Loving your enemies will always be a requirement and many enemies will remain enemies even in the face of your love, but many will turn out to be allies—even family— you didn't know you had. After the dark night of mortal struggle, you might even come to see that the persistent enemy who never ceased to resist you was a vital spark that catalyzed your own redemption.

# Learn to like to work and enjoy the satisfaction of doing your job as well as it can be done

DOC FOUNDED THE Teton Valley Boys Ranch in the 1960s on the idea that work was inherently valuable and that boys needed to learn to like it. It wasn't a camp for troubled kids, even though many parents sent their struggling boys there in the hope that the experience would transform them. It was an unusual experiment. He wanted to ennoble physical work as a kind of service. Some of the work we did—such as painting a widow's house or moving pipe for a local farmer—was directly intended to be an act of service for those in need, but much of it was the kind of work that was required in order to make the camp run and to live as a community. We washed dishes, cooked meals, did laundry, weeded the garden, chopped down trees and built fences out of them, and otherwise cared for the property. It was an experiment in a kind of communal living. I learned more about my responsibilities to others through this work than anything else I had ever experienced. And I learned to love the physical effort it took to do these things well. Our work was regularly inspected. We wanted the pride of knowing we had done things well. He wasn't an onerous task master. I have often reflected on this. I don't know how he extracted so much effort from us, but I think it had something to do with his high ideals. Rather than shaming us for poor work, he simply held us to a standard of excellence and taught us all the good reasons why we should hold ourselves to those same standards. It wasn't for money. You simply didn't want to let him down. And maybe it was our age, as growing adolescent boys, but the physical transformation we could see in our bodies was also exciting. I came home more sinewy and strong, more fit and happy in my own young body.

I don't know why girls were not included in Doc's objectives. He never spoke about this, as far as I know. Certainly there was only so much he could do with one ranch and one idea, but his successor and one of my heroes, Dick Jacobsen, bought the property years later and reinstituted the boys ranch and then created a girls and family ranch on the other side of Teton Valley that my own daughter and then our whole family had the privilege of attending. Around the same time the Birch Creek Service Ranch for boys and girls was founded on the same ideals as the Bennion Boys Ranch by the Peterson family who had worked closely with Doc. Having sent my children to both places, I can attest to the inspiring and transformative opportunities they provide for young people to discover their talents, to learn to love work, and to enjoy their responsibility toward others. No doubt somewhere Doc is smiling.

Doc had written a dissertation on the philosophy of Max Weber and was, I suppose, attracted to the notion of the Protestant work ethic. Because of my exposure to Doc's ranch, many years later as I read Wendell Berry's devastating critique of the denigration of work and of the body in *The Unsettling of America*, I instinctively recognized this as the sermon Doc had been giving, almost without words, at the ranch. Berry suggests that modern life is based on a profound distrust and embarrassment about the limitations of the body. Our technology has enabled us to become less and less dependent on the land and on the labors of our own hands. Consequently, all we can do anymore to make use of our bodies is to beautify them, adorn and worship them. We stay in shape for reasons of vanity and because our bodies have simply lost purpose in modern economies. Of course, he was speaking of the American middle class in particular, since such criticism does not describe the life of the working class and the world's poor. But it is telling that manual labor has lost dignity in modern societies even at the same time as we have worshipped the beautiful body—not the useful one but the one pleasing to stare at. Although increasingly secular, it is as if our society has become even more puritanically embarrassed by the more mundane and biological facts of our embodied nature.

Doc never said much about whether he attached a particularly Mormon spin to the idea of work, but it is not hard to imagine that Doc saw work as redemptive.

And that seems particularly Mormon, or at least charac-
teristic of Christian theologies that see the Fall as a fortunate event, as a fall into blessedness. Surviving by the
sweat of our brow, tilling the soil, and bearing and raising children in physical struggle might seem like curses,
but in such theology, they are blessings, opportunities
to find our redemption in finding our embodied purpose. Doc used to say that prisoners ought to work
and serve not as punishment, but as opportunities to
experience empowerment and selflessness. He never
wanted to give up on people, which is why he also op-
posed capital punishment. The most religious idea associated with work I remember Doc teaching was his
take on the Bhagavad Gita: "To action alone hast thou
a right, not to its fruits." This is heretical to the dogma
of the American Dream, of course. Doc meant by
this that it was hubris to expect specific consequences
from my labors—there was wisdom and humility in accepting the fact that consequences had less to do with
me and more with circumstance, grace, serendipity
perhaps, and certainly the collective work of others. I
think I hear echoes of Doc's thinking in Massachusetts
Senator Elizabeth Warren when she reminds us that
the so-called "self-made man" is more dependent on
the labor of others than he would like us to believe. In
its emphasis on the holiness of the body, the holiness
of physical experience, and the divine potential of all
human endeavors, LDS belief is about as work- and
body-friendly as beliefs come, but it is also true that

the seductions of capitalism have led us to neglect the communitarian work ethic of the beehive with which the LDS religion began. Work, for Doc, had to have a purpose beyond self-interest; its greatest objective was to forget oneself on behalf of others and on behalf of something larger than oneself.

Doc never used the language of getting ahead, pulling oneself up by the bootstraps, or becoming the self-made man. I was always struck by the differences between Doc's ideas and the more typical language about the American Dream that I heard in my church upbringing. I suppose by some definitions, my grandfather was a self-made man. He grew up a somewhat destitute farmer and brick mason in Salt Lake valley only to become an MBA and a successful banker in New York City in the middle of the Great Depression. This in turn allowed my father to seek even more educational opportunities in his life and put me in a position of privilege to be able to choose the life of the mind. Which is why it is hard for me, I guess, to describe my life as self-made, no matter how hard I have worked to achieve my own dreams. My contemporary life was built on the foundations laid by those who have come before me and certainly not just family members but school teachers, church leaders, civic leaders, and even the working classes who built my homes, repaired my plumbing, and paved my streets.

My grandfather was a peer of Doc's and knew him and encouraged my participation at the ranch. Having grown up poor and on a farm as the oldest child and having lost his father early in a car accident, my grandfather knew how to work physically hard and appreciated others who did as well, but it was hard not to feel in the American middle class and Christian culture I grew up in that American progress meant that we should ultimately strive to leave manual work behind. Having been raised in a wealthy community in Connecticut, I was grateful for my parents and for Doc who taught me to avoid the assumption that there was something undignified about those who preferred simple, low-paying professions—such as artists or educators—or working with their hands—such as carpenters and builders—and least of all about those who appeared unable to extract themselves from a blue collar world.

For Doc, the value of work was in the act of submission to a process of making that consumed us and that enjoined us to one another and to the world, as well as forged a union of body and spirit. For Doc, every job required skills and every job done well required an accomplishment akin to art. You knew you were succeeding in the task when you found yourself gaining aptitude and efficiency as you lost a consciousness of the difficulty of the work and let instinct take over. This is when you found yourself falling into a kind of rhythm with the tools and materials in your hands. And this was not usually achieved on an individual basis merely; work was a collective effort and it was always valuable in a relational context. As I think back on those years at the ranch, I knew something was happening when a group of boys would begin making up songs, jokes, or legends associated with the work in question and when they began to see themselves as working as a collective whole. Eventually a kind of internally driven but shared competitiveness would take over, just for the pride and pleasure of seeing how well the work could be done. And as the summer wore on, our bodies as well as our environments were mutually transformed.

I wasn't exactly a city slicker, even though that was what one of the local ranchers liked to call us, but the transition from upper middle class suburbia to a western ranch for the summer was a significant cultural change. I suppose my friends wondered if I had done something wrong to deserve to be sent off to the wilds of Idaho to work on a ranch. What they didn't know was the best kept secret of the camp. We had to work twenty hours a week, every week morning for four hours, and the rest of the time was spent in Teton Valley—one of the most beautiful places in America—hiking, fishing, jumping on the trampoline, horseback riding, and holding evening discussions, debates, and skits—learning to like all the other things Doc spoke of. And we got a pay check at the end of the summer for our labors. It didn't matter that the $50 I received at the conclusion of the summer was not a lot of money, only $.63 an hour as I now calculate it; I have never experienced quite the same sense of satisfaction in earning so little.

We were put on different work crews, usually for an entire week, and this gave us an opportunity to learn new skills, to work with a different set of boys and counselors. I yearned for the chance to weed with Doc in the garden, but once I did, I discovered he was not much for conversation. He was normally not all that talkative, but in the garden he focused almost zen-like on the tasks at hand. So it turned me away from my ever busy imagination and helped me to learn to forget myself and forget my dreams of what Adam Miller, in his wonderful essay on "Groundhog Day," has called a "frictionless" world. Miller writes:

> *Heaven? Where people are still married, still work, still have children, still change diapers, still share casseroles? Heaven, for Mormons, is what seals our union with the mundane rather than terminates it. Leave it to Mormonism to see the nihilistic claim that there is nothing but the aching specificity of this repetition and raise it to the power of infinity. Leave it to Mormonism to claim that even in heaven we'll have to button and unbutton our shirts, show all our work, suffer paper cuts, and—of course, forever and ever gain—breathe.* (123)

I know Doc used to say that as he grew closer to death, he was less interested in heaven and salvation and more interested in simply continuing the work he had already begun. I might have winced hearing him say this, because at that point in my life heaven was just beginning to become a real desire of my heart. I wanted to hear him say that yes, indeed, heaven was worth pursuing because of how different and how much better it would be than here. But I now see that Doc didn't mean anything heretical by this. Quite the opposite, because he understood that heaven's use to us is to get our heads up from the trough of life long enough to see that earth work is what we should most desire. To paraphrase Robert Frost's peerless poem, "Birches," sometimes we need to get away from life for a while only to discover that earth's the right place for us. What Christianity for so long thought signaled our alienation from God—our bodies and the messy conditions of this world that require sweat and pain and sorrow and effort—were all along the means of our salvation and the very substance of our heaven.

# Learn to like the song of birds, the companionship of dogs

I LIKE TO MOUNTAIN BIKE and I often go with my friend Darren and his dog Theo. Theo is a springer spaniel, a brown burst of muscle and animal joy. He can barely contain himself when Darren pulls into the parking lot at the trailhead. He jumps out of the car and runs in frantic circles. He greets me every time but never stays close enough to me for much of a petting session. He is too wiggly and too joyous to take the time for a friendly pat on the head or a scratch under his chin. When he senses that Darren is ready to get on his bike, or if he feels that Darren is taking too long to get ready, he will begin to stand on his hind legs and bark as if his head were ready to explode. Darren gently chides him, "alright, alright, we are going. Sheesh!" Once we are off, usually starting uphill, he runs to and fro, back and forth, covering easily two or three times the distance we do as he jumps into the bushes or frolics through the ferns, barking at pretend enemies or sniffing out hideouts of rabbits. When I first started riding with Theo, he made me nervous. I was afraid that I would hit him as he wove in and out between us, but I soon learned that his timing and athleticism are impeccable. He never missteps.

When we start to head downhill, he bolts as fast as he can to keep up. If the trail is straight enough, it becomes difficult for him to stay beside us. I have sometimes found myself gliding downhill and I look over and see his joyful embrace of life, while his tongue hangs out to one side, and I have thought he is the quintessence of earthly joy. He certainly knows what happiness is. For him it is the freedom of a trail and the companionship of Darren. I was recently flyfishing on the Provo and as I rounded a bend, I saw a dog at a distance sitting on a rock, like a wet rag. He barked at me in recognition. It was Theo, playing in the river with Darren's daughters. He was happy to see me. I felt flattered that he could recognize me from so far away. As I drew closer, he was eager to come and greet me.

I don't know why it is that Theo moves me so much. I think it is his animal joy. His simplicity. And his headlong embrace of the chance to run in the mountains, to work himself to a well-earned rest, and the pleasure of rolling in the grass, the dirt, or on a good day, in the mud. He reminds me of something about myself I can too easily forget—that I too am animal and I too find instinctive pleasure and joy in free movement in the outdoors. I always want to have his capacity to relish this earthly life and its sensuous pleasures as long as I am able. I want to feel the exhaustion of my body after a good hike, the pleasure of the sights and smells of the hills, and I want to be able to express my pleasure without embarrassment. Walt Whitman called it his "barbaric yawp." Sometimes a whelp, a whoop, a holler are just what the doctor ordered, and I think that if it weren't for dogs, we might forget this great joy of the earth.

I love too that his name is Theo. His name means God. I joke about it with Darren. Just mix up the lettering and a dog is a god. God is a God of flesh and bone. His Son was incarnated here on this earth in a body just like yours and mine. Animal in its root meaning implies spirit and spirituality. There is a holiness to the fleshly exultations of Theo. I believe earthly joy in the presence of those we love, in the warmth and comfort of close relationships, and in the presence of natural beauty is one of the holiest feelings available to us. I suppose animals have a lot to teach us in this regard.

For allergy reasons, I am not currently a pet owner, but I grew up with dogs and a cat. And my earliest contact with any wild animal was the experience of fishing with my grandfather on the Provo River. I remember the smell of the water, the electric feel of a live fish gasping for breath in my hand, and the smell of cleaning and cooking a trout. To this day, there is scarcely any memory from my childhood as vivid as those times with my grandfather learning about the intelligence of these animals that lay just beneath the surface of the water but who managed to be invisible and elusive all the same. Until I ate my own fish, I had never really connected what I ate to the life of the earth.

I was a suburbanite, so it wasn't until my experiences at the Boys Ranch that I truly immersed myself in the world of domesticated animals, particularly the world of horses, pigs, and occasionally goats and sheep. I was terrified to learn to ride a horse. My uncle John owned a beautiful Palomino that was housed in Lehi. He occasionally took us to his horse to feed him when we were in town. At the ranch, though, I learned to ride. And it was a man by the name of Art Kearsley who taught us.

I can't adequately paint a picture of Art, but he was an old timer who teased us "city slickers" for not having the least bit of common sense. He was usually right. He never remembered any of our names, so he usually called us either Oscar or Pete. But he knew his horses' names and there were many of them. And he entrusted this young group of ill-trained boys to ride with him through the woods above the ranch. We walked a lot but every so often we would trot and then gallop. I have a distinct memory of galloping well beyond my pay grade as a horseman. I was hanging onto the saddle in desperation as my feet had come loose in the stirrups, and I looked up just in time to see a tree branch hanging right in my path. I ducked and avoided certain decapitation as we flew through a beautiful aspen grove. I started to laugh uncontrollably as I awkwardly bounced in the saddle. I was both

terrified and utterly joyful at the same time. This animal beneath me had a personality, a will of her own,
and the world around me was living and breathing.
That was perhaps the greatest gift of the ranch for
a young boy: the chance to understand yourself in
companionship of live things. Too much of my world
was predictable, mechanized, or sheltered from the
elements. I see this now, fully recognizing that the
kind of childhood I enjoyed was far more immersed
in the animal world than the kind of childhood most
people have today. I could explore a creek in my backyard in Connecticut. I caught salamanders under the
blackened leaves and mulch. I caught minnows in the
stream and built forts from the roots of fallen trees. I
caught snappers in the estuaries from the Long Island
Sound and caught clams and crabs on the beach.

I was recently in Chile in the forests of the Lake
District, which are filled with enormous hardwood
trees. I could hear birdsong I had never heard before. One of the birds sounded like a lost child in the
woods, so plaintive and haunting that it caused me to
look around just in case there was someone nearby
who was calling for help. I could hear the sounds of
some species of woodpeckers doing their work among
the trees. The buzzing insects and sounds of the wind
among the trees reminded me of what I experienced
for the first time in the high mountains of the Tetons
those many summers ago: that feeling that I was in the
midst of a vast and unknown and diverse community,

only passing through, and that I didn't matter one bit to this community. It would go on communing, interacting, and regenerating life without me. It would be able to do so much better in fact without me. I don't say that out of misanthropy for what it means to be a human. I think it is our greatest privilege as humans to experience our own nothingness and a deep sense of awe and reverence for the independence of the world and its creatures. We too are creatures. We too are a bit of the divine in the flesh and our experience of the body and of plant and animal life are a miracle and a gift beyond measure. I remember seeing a video of Lowell Bennion giving what was his only talk in a General Conference meeting. It was a General Priesthood meeting. This is what he said:

> *Until a year or two ago I kept a pig. My pig never got his eyes above the trough, except when I came to feed him; and, brethren, when I went out to feed my pig, I thrilled at the color on Mt. Olympus, and I pondered its geology, and I worshiped at the foot of the mountain. I sang "O Ye Mountains High" to myself alone, and "For the Strength of the Hills." I like animals, but believe me, I am grateful for those qualities which are distinctly human and which are divine.* (1968)

I had fed the pigs many times at the ranch. I knew what he meant. And I wondered too if my own animal existence couldn't be more meaningful if I could couple the joys of an embodied life with the work of self-reflection and self-conscious understanding. We can get it wrong. We can be all animal and lose self-conscious awareness and never see ourselves for what we are. Or we can become all spirit, all self-reflection and never learn to lose ourselves in the work and love of this life. Awe and wonder are our privilege but they are a gift precisely because of the way they surprise us and awaken us in our animal existence.

# Learn to like gardening, puttering around the house, and fixing things

I SPEAK WITH NO AUTHORITY on this principle. I am a very unsuccessful gardener even though I like to blame the fact that my yard doesn't get enough sun to grow things, and I am a far cry from a handy man. I don't feel any particular pride even in my ability to keep a yard. I feel a great deal of shame about this and envy those with more skill and aptitude than I have. I know I could place a higher priority on domestic responsibilities, but I also try to blame my busy life. But that is Doc's point, isn't it? I can't even really blame my upbringing: sure, my father wasn't much of a handy man himself, but I worked hard throughout my youth mowing lawns, weeding yards and gardens, and doing restaurant work. I am good for a project as a helper; just don't ask me to be in charge and expect me to know what to do. I am quick to forget things I learn, especially when the practice goes dormant for long periods of time. And passing through graduate school while raising a young family and moving from apartment to apartment, I didn't own much of anything to make or keep up a home until I was into my thirties. And at that point, all of my discipline was focused on trying to get parenting right, being a decent husband, serving in my church, and writing and teaching. I later added a host of civic responsibilities. I learned to swim in swift currents. The only remnant skill that has never left me is that I am a killer dishwasher. I love doing the dishes and generally do them every day. I love tackling massive amounts of them, and I never want or need any help. Not much of a virtue, I know.

I know lots of self-taught sprinkler repairmen, car mechanics, and home builders. I learned from sad experience early in my life that I was more likely to make things worse when attempting major, or sometimes even minor, home projects. I take things apart and then have no idea how to put them back together, and I am the worst reader and follower of instructions. For example, we are devotees of complex board games in my household (you know the ones— the Catan series, Seven Wonders, Dominion, and the like), but don't expect me to ever read and understand how to play a game. Don't even bother explaining the rules to me because they won't be well assimilated. Just let me play along a round of two and I will have the game figured out by then. I might even beat you. Fortunately, my wife is expert at reading complex instructions and never forgets rules. But if more than a month passes and I haven't played the game for 100 or more hours, I won't remember how to play. Not a thing. It almost feels like a disability, but I learn almost entirely by intuition. Get me playing again, and it all comes back.

It may be that Doc is speaking from a later stage of life that is more conducive to home projects than the one I find myself in now, but the point he is making is pretty simple. I think it is best understood in his use of the word "puttering." To putter around the house is to move about in a relaxed manner, feeling no particular rush or anxiety, to engage in a series of tasks—cleaning, repairing, improving—that are not monumental but still vital to the economic engine of a home. It implies a general approach to life that doesn't take things too seriously, that enjoys existence itself, and that knows how to balance the life of Martha with the life of Mary.

I see this as a two-fold principle: 1) SLOW DOWN, make time for and learn to enjoy mundane tasks as ends in themselves and 2) learn economic independence and maybe even a modicum of moral independence by acquiring domestic skills; quit farming out your responsibilities. On this second point, Doc used to say that one should learn at least one fundamental and marketable skill, like plumbing or home construction (maybe today we could add web design), that would not only help to save money and increase self-reliance but also serve as a personal safety net. This is one way to achieve greater independence from a globalized and overly bureaucratized economy.

On the first point, perhaps you are not as guilty as I am, but I know deep down that if I just gave my home greater attention and a higher priority, I would discover that I am not as clumsy or slow to learn as I like to think I am. I am committed to return to the quest of being a better gardener. When Amy and I were first married and living in graduate student housing, we rented a plot of ground that was part of a communal garden. We had enormous success, growing more tomatoes and zucchini that we could ever use, and this forced us to be creative in making soups and salsas and other dishes that we could share generously with others. We often saw our neighbors out in the garden with their children, doing as we were doing, and it felt like real joy. Our collective abandonment of gardening as a national culture, as well as our neglect of it in recent years as a religious culture, has no excuse. Considering the enormous distances that food must travel these days and at such tremendous cost in energy consumption, packaging and waste, and in land use, the eating-local ethos is much needed. Over the years, we have joined a few community shared agriculture projects and have enjoyed the challenge of finding ways to cook goods of the earth with which we are largely unfamiliar. I wonder why we champion self-reliance as a virtue in our culture without stressing the value of producing our own food as families and as communities.

I think I spent the better part of the first half of my married life (having just passed the twenty-eight year mark) rushing, rushing, rushing. I maintained a laser-like focus on completing the landmarks of an academic life, all while trying desperately to be an available and giving husband and father, giving all that was asked of me in a lay church for many hours every week, and being an active citizen, what the LDS scriptures call being "actively engaged in a good cause" (D&C 58:27). I have learned that each of these areas of responsibility can swallow the others all by themselves, but other than a firm commitment to doing the dishes every night, doing the minimal amount of work on the lawn and yard, changing the oil in my cars, and occasionally washing them, and doing the most basic repair work, sometimes only after repeated prodding from my wife, what can I say about my work spent on the home? I have spent the last several years trying desperately to simplify, cut back, say no to excess commitments, and so far I have only small pieces of evidence that I am starting to live a less stressful life, one that involves a little more puttering and a little less panic and rush.

Maybe puttering is a little bit misleading since taking on more responsibilities in the home can mean a lot more work. My wife and I agreed that our anniversary gift to each other a few years ago would be a household project to tear up the hideous outdoor carpet on our backyard patio and to lay down some tile, something we had never done and were intent on learning ourselves. The carpet was torn up, the surface of the cement patio prepared, and the tile purchase arrived. A few weeks later and every spare moment had been spent in exhausting work. But with her abilities to read and assimilate instructions and my obedient brawn, it turned out to be a very romantic gift indeed. Such work won't save my soul, and it won't rescue me from me from an economy that has me in its ever-tightening grasp of dependency, but it is a needed step in the right direction.

# Learn to like the sunrise and sunset, the beating of rain on the roof and windows, and the gentle fall of snow on a winter day

*Between the vision of the Tourist Board and the true*
*Paradise lies the desert where Isaiah's elations*
*force a rose from the sand.*

—*Derek Walcott*

THESE LINES FROM "THE BOUNTY" by the St. Lucian poet Derek Walcott have inspired me for many years (3). They articulate for me what is an important principle that resonates with what Doc here is teaching. Walcott here suggests that there are two idealized, air-brushed versions of our environment, one that offers only the beauty of a place at its most exceptional, perhaps in the form of a postcard or an Instagram post and the other, the mental image we all carry of what paradise might be, whether that is the image of the garden from which we were expelled or the paradise to which we hope to return. In either case, the ordinary reality of this world always looks cheap by comparison since we can only notice what it lacks. The actual and ordinary place where we live in this world at this moment—what Walcott here calls the "desert"— is always compared to the extraordinary or the ideal and continually comes up wanting. But then Walcott suggests that maybe we can learn a thing or two from the artists, the poet-prophets who can see more deeply what is before them. He suggests that what makes the desert blossom as a rose is not some act of engineering that would convert a brown place, an unruly place, into some ordered and green garden, but is instead an act of poetic appreciation that sees the beauty in the mundane.

In 2009 Gary Barton, an art professor at BYU, and I brought a group of students to the Caribbean to study the poetry and the home landscape of Walcott, one of the world's greatest living poets. Walcott was born and raised in the small island of St. Lucia in the Caribbean, and while you and I might think of his home landscape as exceptional and exotic, he was educated in a colonial school that taught him about the greatness of the British and European landscapes by the great Western masters of landscape art and of British romantic poetry. All of that exposure almost explicitly seemed to condemn his tropical landscape for being too unruly, barbaric, and unordered. Walcott devoted his life to rescuing the beauty of his island from this kind of condemnation as well as from the ways in which tourism has exoticized his landscape to the point where it is presented as the environmental equivalent of an airbrushed pinup photo. What he prefers is what he calls the "awe of the ordinary," the capacity of the

artist's eye to find wonder and appreciation in the quiet
and hot afternoons when local villagers are seen mill-
ing about in the streets, when the rain pours in buckets,
drumming loudly on the roofs of corrugated tin and
then clears just as suddenly, leaving the streets steam-
ing in the hot sun (*Tiepolo's Hound* 8). Having served
my mission in the Caribbean basin, in Venezuela, I had
come to appreciate these kinds of routine experiences.
I loved walking the streets at twilight, seeing the smoke
from the houses rising in the disappearing light, stray
dogs wandering the streets, and the sound of music
and chatter in the air.

Loving a place requires an all-inclusive love, an un-
conditional fondness even for the sometimes boring or
otherwise unremarkable moments when the skies are
gray, when the rain drizzles, or when we find ourselves
between seasons. That, anyway, is what I have learned
from Walcott about how to live here in the American
West. Even this western landscape where I live, as
beautiful as it seems to me now on a daily basis, has
been seen historically through the lens of Eastern bias
as lacking sufficient water, greenery, trees. Too much
brown. Too much openness. And of course it is too
arid. It certainly felt that way the first time I saw it,
and it has struggled ever since white men arrived here
to get out from under the weight of expectations—
shaped by generations of those who came from the
British Isles, from Scandinavia, and from New England—to have more grass, more trees, and more water

than the ecology of this semi-arid desert could provide. Wallace Stegner once said that if you are going to live in the West, you are going to have to get over the color green. Certainly what this requires, then, is not so much greater engineering of the landscape to make it conform to our expectations, but rather a greater humility and deeper appreciation for its own bounteous gifts. The desert is already always blossoming. It already has its own unique colors, moods, and subtle beauty. Once you have the eyes to see, this place needs no apologies on its behalf. It needs instead the equivalent of "Isaiah's elations" in response the gift of its bounty. It deserves the highest attention of art. And there is a lesson here too not just for Westerners but for all of us. With the eyes to see and appreciate beauty and bounty in the ordinary moments of physical life, we are in such a more powerful position to appreciate mortality itself, the passage of time, the particulars of our own ordinary and special lives, and the wonder of existence. The great author Dostoevsky, whose own life was almost cut short by a firing squad only to then receive pardon, learned what a gift his life was. He devoted much of his artistic gifts to try to stress the need for all of us to awaken—spiritually and aesthetically—to the awe of this life, so that even one day would be sufficient to experience all joy. Once possessed of this understanding, we would find that this life could be paradise enough.

In St. Lucia, our students were taught to see a Caribbean that lay beyond the postcard image of the place, to see it through the eyes of art. What they saw was both uglier, coarser, more variable and more mundane but ultimately far more rewarding. We spent our days painting on hillsides and beaches and on street corners in fishing villages. We ate at local bakeries and fish shops. We lived in the neighborhood. Of course, our time was limited, but we gained a relationship to the people, their history, and to the place that helped us to see more beneath the surface of things. At the conclusion of our time in St. Lucia, we met with Walcott at his house where he entertained us for the evening. He was intent that we stay to the end of the day and watch as the sun set before us. His house was perched on a small overlook above the Caribbean Sea facing the western sunset. As the sun dropped on the horizon, the colors deepened, the mood relaxed, and we sat astonished at a display of light we had never seen before, just as the sun finally disappeared below the horizon. Walcott recited favorite French poetry as we watched the light flare and then dissipate.

There is some risk in sharing this experience because of its implication that you and I need to go to distant and exotic locales to experience beauty more deeply, but it might be helpful to remember that this was Walcott's home, his birthplace, and while he had the fame to live just about anywhere in the world, he chose to remain on his small, native island—a place that for all its exotic appeal is also easily characterized as a provincial backwater. Nevertheless, even into his eighties before he died, he never tired of the ordinary streets of his own island. As he once put it, "so much to do still, all of it praise" (*White Egrets* 86).

You and I have our own paradises that we neglect at our own peril. We might suffer from idealized images of what the world should look like, but part of what distracts us these days from appreciating the ordinary moments is also our overscheduled busyness and our attention taken up by social media, smart phones, entertainment, and commercialism. We are suffering what the great poet and philosopher Octavio Paz called "aesthetic impoverishment" (144). We don't know how to appreciate simple beauty because we rely too much on others to tell us what to like, what to pay attention to, and what to value. And those "others" are most likely brilliant marketers, politicians, and entertainers who vie for our attention. And what we value is what we spend our time and our money on—what we give our full attention to. When we consider the doctrinal foundations of the creation, it is not overstatement to say that inattention to the wonder of the creation and the sheer miracle of the passage of time in these bodies on this earth dishonors the creator. Adam and Eve were given the creation to be used, but more importantly to be wondered at. The Lord explains the simple wonder of a tree: "And out of the ground made I, the Lord God, to grow every tree, naturally, that is pleasant

to the sight of man; and man could behold it. And it
became also a living soul" (Moses 3:9).

Have we the foggiest idea what this means? Have
we given any serious consideration to the fact that
when we observe this world and encounter the ordinary materiality of our day-to-day lives, we are encoun-
tering a myriad of living souls, not merely in the miraculous faces of our fellow humans but in the presence
of trees, wind, clouds, mountains, animals, and insects?
"And man could behold it." Are we wonderers? Do
we ever find ourselves staring at the most mundane of
things around us in simple astonishment? Adam and
Eve's wonder in the face of creation was likely stimu-
lated by the fact that they had no preconceptions of
what it was that they might be looking at. They weren't
looking for anything in particular or looking past what
was before them. They were simply beholding and be-
holden to the world. And this, of course, is the great
quest of all art, to tear us away from our ingrained habits of seeing, of paying attention to what we have already learned is worth paying attention to, and thereby
missing virtually the entirety of what it is that stands
before us. Children see like artists, which is why a twig,
a rock, a broken bird's wing—all of it can become a
cause for wonder, for preservation, and care.

The oceans regulate the climate on this planet. The
atmosphere, the weather, the rotation of the earth and
the rising and the sinking of the sun, everything that
allows us to move and have our being, is the gift of

biology, which is also, if we are to listen to King Benjamin, a gift of God's grace. If we see with the eyes of love and gratitude, every sunset, every rain storm, and even every gray day will seem more miraculous. Such power of perception has to be the most clean and renewable resource we have.

# Learn to keep your wants simple and refuse to be controlled by the likes and dislikes of others

WHAT I HAVE ALWAYS FOUND INTRIGUING about Doc's thinking and his many books is that they are so utterly commonsensical that their importance is almost too easily lost on us. He kept his wants, his principles, and his thinking simple. And yet, like all great ideas, although they are presented in simple and straightforward language, they hold up against increased scrutiny and probing, revealing more rather than less. In the case of this, his final aphorism, Doc might as well have quoted from the Savior, "where your treasure is, there will your heart be also" (Matthew 6:21) or from the familiar Mormon children's song with its simple declaration, "I am a child of God."

To simplify our wants brings us back to his first principle, which was to learn to like what doesn't cost much. But he adds here a social and psychological dimension to our behavior as consumers, helping us to see more comprehensively that what we consume, what we work for, aspire to, and dream of—if we are not careful—can be controlled by what we perceive to be the expectations of others. In other words, while we might have thought that simplification is merely a refusal to be seduced by commercialization, Doc here suggests that at root what we desire from life stems from how we conceive of ourselves and how we understand ourselves in relation to others. Commercialization, after all, works because it plays our desires against others, putting us into a cage of competition to get what others are getting before it runs out.

This clearly extends well beyond what we might normally call "peer pressure." It has as much or more to do with those expectations and pressures that we internalize and normalize almost without thought that are simply part of our social and cultural environments, those habits of thought that have led us to believe, for example, that material possessions themselves hold some intrinsic value for the possessor, that physical beauty grants superiority to its possessor, or that such things as material gain, political advantage, and social difference sustained by habits, social norms, and even by institutions or laws, provide adequate measures of our worth. It might not even matter anymore who first put us on the treadmill of vanity, since we are the ones willingly and frantically pushing ourselves to run faster in place. If an anthropologist from Mars were to arrive in the midst of our lives and see what it is we spend the most time and money and effort in order to gain, would those observations not reveal the nature of our deepest attachments and the real god that we worship? Do we not learn something fundamental about our ideas of ourselves and our self-worth when we examine what it is we most desire and spend most of our time obtaining? Which begs the question: for which mess of pottage have we willingly traded our inherent worth? What have we allowed to distract us from discovering the simplicity and marvel of our most fundamental gifts: the chance to come to know, love, and serve other people; the privilege of relishing the beauties and bounties of nature; the opportunity to work, develop, and learn; and the chance merely to experience and relish existence?

I am not an expert, but I have read enough psychology and Dostoevsky to understand that we learn early in life by imitation and conformity but also by intentional differentiation and resistance. We learn to become who we are precisely on the basis of the relationships of family, friends, and lovers and what we learn extends into who we are as citizens, consumers, employees, and neighbors. We learn early on how to anticipate and perhaps even to shape reactions in others. We test our limits against those of others. We want to know where the boundaries are. We need to know wherein our freedom lies, but almost as soon as we discover it, it is as if we can barely stand to have it. So we often use our freedom precisely to destroy it. We are often more than happy to make concessions that will lift the burdens and responsibilities that come with our freedom. Let someone else tell us what to do, how to think, what to value. Let others program our lives, determine our worth, and prophesy our future, since the uncertainties of life, the mixed results of our achievements, and the imperfect satisfactions we find are simply too much for us to bear.

What is it that might prevent this abdication of freedom? I believe it is charity, what the LDS scriptures additionally call "the pure love of Christ" (Moroni 7:47). This is the capacity to bear all things, endure all things, to be forbearing, patient in suffering, and uncompromising in the love we offer to others. Charity means being content, as Paul says, not only with the fundamental material needs but also with the fact that "everywhere and in all things I am instructed both to be full and to be hungry, both to abound and to suffer need" (Philippians 4:12). Life is never perfectly smooth. It never brings us exactly what we want. We should learn to strive for improvement of our circumstances but we must also learn perpetual contentment with where and what we are. Nothing other than charity will prove more effectual in resisting the charms, illusions, and vanities that appear to be promised to us on the condition that we simply conform to the likes and dislikes of others. This capacity, however, is not a natural gift. It cannot be bought. It cannot be wrested from God. But it can and should be wanted, according to the Book of Mormon prophet, "with all the energy of heart" (Moroni 7:48). And it is bestowed on those who pray and plead for it, who, if we are to listen to the principles of the Sermon on

the Mount, are those who understand their own in-
sufficiencies with perfect clarity. That is, they know
what *they don't have* and instead of turning to the world
to supply their needs, they turn to God. Not so that
he will complete them with material things but so that
he will give them the capacity to see their insufficiency
as a state of blessedness. These are not the strong but
the meek, not those who believe in what they have at-
tained but the poor in spirit who see what they have
failed to find, those who are unsatisfied by the illusions and vanities of this life. We can only come to a
deeper happiness, in other words, through a learned
patience with sorrow and dissatisfaction. The phrase
"the pure love of Christ" has the double meaning of
his pure love for us and our pure love for him. In other
words, our capacity to keep our wants simple and to
not be controlled by the likes and dislikes of others is
as much a function of our capacity to feel and accept
Christ's pure love for us as it is our willingness to strive
to obtain and demonstrate that love for him. When
we have finally learned to want what is best designed
for our deepest happiness, Mormon promises, we will
"see him as he is" (Moroni 7:48). We must begin, then,
by striving to emulate Christ as a model of living that
is higher and more valuable than what we see around
us. Of course, until we know him more intimately this
might begin with nothing more than a desire to believe
there is something higher than the world and social
relations in which we find ourselves. But with time,

his atonement changes us. We not only want to see a higher reality but we begin to inhabit it and can see the vanities of this life more clearly. In this way, instead of casting us out of reality, our faith in Christ ultimately helps us to become more authentically ourselves.

This is perhaps the great secret behind Doc's aphorisms. Although they do not explicitly mention Christ or his atonement, they do describe the transformative power of partnering our desires with God so as to "learn to like" what is higher, better, and more worthy of our affections. Such work is life-long and it is never easy. Because it involves submission, sacrifice, and discipline, it is also deeply religious in character. The great promise is that with time and the rituals of practice, we are able to start to see ourselves as agents who are in the process of gaining a margin of freedom over our natural and circumstantially-induced tendencies. Learning to like in new ways is the path to becoming a new creature, of having a new heart, of being born again. Life is sweet to the newborn babe who finds herself in loving arms, but life is sweetest to the mature adult for whom life has become the fruit of her own choosing.

# Books by Lowell Bennion

(1939). *Youth and Its Religion*. Salt Lake City: Mutual Improvement Association of the LDS Church.

(1940). *The Religion of the Latter-day Saints*. Salt Lake City: LDS Dept. of Education.

(1955). *An Introduction to the Gospel*. Salt Lake City: Deseret Sunday School Union Board.

(1956). *Teachings of the New Testament (2nd ed.)*. Salt Lake City: Deseret Book.

(1959). *Religion and the Pursuit of Truth*. Salt Lake City: Deseret Book.

(1978). *Things That Matter Most. Salt Lake City:* Bookcraft.

(1985). *The Book of Mormon: A Guide to Christian Living*. Salt Lake City: Deseret Book.

(1988). England, Eugene, ed. *The Best of Lowell L. Bennion: Selected Writings 1928–1988*. Salt Lake City: Deseret Book.

(1990). *Legacies of Jesus*. Salt Lake City: Deseret Book.

(1996). *How Can I Help?: Final Selections By the Legendary Writer, Teacher, and Humanitarian*. Salt Lake City: Aspen Books.

# Works Cited

Bennion, Lowell. "Seek Ye Wisdom" (1968). http://scriptures.byu.edu/gettalk.php?ID=1619.

Brown, William P. *The Seven Pillars of Creation: The Bible, Science, and the Ecology of Wonder.* Oxford: Oxford University Press, 2010.

Kelson, Aaron. *The Holy Place: Why Caring for the Earth and Being Kind to Animals Matters.* Spotsylvania, VA: White Pine Publishing, 1999.

Miller, Adam. *Rube Goldberg Machines: Essays in Mormon Theology.* Salt Lake City: Greg Kofford Books, 2012.

Paz, Octavio. *The Other Voice: Essays on Modern Poetry.* New York: Harvest Books, 1992.

Robinson, Marilynne. "The Radiant Astonishment of Existence: Two Interviews with Marilynne Robinson, March 20, 2004 and February 9, 2007." By George Handley and Lance Larsen. *Literature and Belief* 27.2 (2007): 113–43.

de Unamuno, Miguel. *The Tragic Sense of Life.* Princeton: Princeton University Press, 1972.

Walcott, Derek. *The Bounty.* New York: Farrar, Straus, and Giroux, 1998.

_____. *Tiepolo's Hound.* New York: Farrar, Straus, and Giroux, 2000.

_____. *White Egrets.* New York: Farrar, Straus, and Giroux, 2011.

# About the Author

A Professor of Interdisciplinary Humanities at Brigham Young University, George B. Handley's creative writing, literary criticism, and civic engagement focus on the intersection between religion, literature, and the environment. A literary scholar and ecocritic whose work is characterized by its comparative reach across the cultures and landscapes of Latin America, the Caribbean, and the United States, he is also known for creative writing that is praised for its eloquence and unique capacity to blend nature writing, theology, and family history. His works include:

*American Fork* (novel)
*Home Waters* (memoir)
*Postcolonial Ecologies* (with Elizabeth DeLoughrey)
*New World Poetics*
*Caribbean Literature and the Environment* (with Elizabeth DeLoughrey & Renée Gosson)
*Stewardship and the Creation* (with Terry Ball & Steven Peck)
*Postslavery Literatures in the Americas*

Find him online at:

http://www.georgebhandley.com/
http://www.patheos.com/blogs/homewaters

Made in United States
Orlando, FL
31 August 2022

21842377R00068